■SCHOLASTIC

# *Quick* Nonfiction Writing Activities That Really Work!

### Marc Tyler Nobleman

NEW YORK • TORONTO • LONDON • AUCKLAND • SYDNEY
MEXICO CITY • NEW DELHI • HONG KONG • BUENOS AIRES

Teaching Resources

To Andrew, whose word is always true.

Edited by Sarah Longhi
Cover design by Jason Robinson
Illustrations by Marc Tyler Nobleman
Interior design by Robert Alemán Design

ISBN-13: 978-0-545-04874-3
ISBN-10: 0-545-04874-5

# Contents

# Introduction

In a batch of thank-you letters I received after one of my school visits, a comment from a girl named Shannon stood out: "My teacher told us you wrote nonfiction, and I thought, 'Oh, no!' But I was wrong!"

I've written books or articles about the creators of Superman, the invention of the telephone, foxes, ghosts, the planets, the Liberty Bell, Kwanzaa, Greece, the history of junk food, the origins of everyday pets, the reasons we laugh, myths about pirates, Rosa Parks, Juan Ponce de León, the Great Chicago Fire, and more. As a whole, those topics don't have much in common, but most of the material I wrote about them does.

In each case, I strove to make my nonfiction come alive. All writers owe it to their readers to do this. If writers are bored when writing, how will readers feel when reading their work? That's a question I don't want my readers to have to answer.

Helping students like Shannon realize that nonfiction means *non*-boring is the focus of this book. And I've written it without saying "Truth is stranger than fiction." For starters, that's a cliché, and clichés, of course, spoil good writing like mold on cream cheese. But more to the point, truth can also be more exciting, scarier, funnier, or sadder than fiction.

## How to Use This Book

This book is designed to provide students the tools to *create* strong nonfiction. Loaded with reproducibles both fun and functional, it breaks down nonfiction to its many components, letting students strengthen their skills one sentence at a time. While the approach includes some grammar, it is largely concerned with content, style, and structure. Sprinkled throughout are "quick tips" for adding a little extra life or lyricism to writing.

Use these pages as they support your students' writing needs and match your writing curriculum. They are perfect for group work of any size and for independent practice. To introduce an activity, you may want to conduct a mini-lesson by reviewing the goal and examples provided and then engage students in guided practice by having them work on one or two items and

**Use the activity pages in the order that best suits your curriculum goals and students' needs.**

then share their work with the group. Students who are ready may complete the rest of the activity independently while students who need more support might work in a small group or directly with you.

Most activities require students to create their own short responses to guided prompts, and therefore, they have no single right answer. A few of the activities, such as Determine the Point of View (page 13) ask students to categorize types of writing or apply grammar rules. At the end of the book, you'll find an answer key with explanations and tips for reviewing this second type of exercise. No matter which activities you assign, be sure to help students reflect and self-assess their work by inviting them to share their answers and ideas. This motivates students to learn from one another and gives you an opportunity to clear up any misconceptions and reteach on the spot when necessary.

## Important Points to Convey to Your Novice Nonfiction Writers

Just because a true story is compelling does not mean it is easy to put into print or memorable once it's in print. One of my professors used to say it's not enough to have a good story. You need a good story, *well told*. Sometimes, a good writer can take even a story that at first seems unremarkable and type gold from it. Often, school writing—responding to assigned prompts or crafting standardized test essays—poses that challenge.

Whether your students are writing descriptive, expository, narrative, or persuasive nonfiction, they are usually assuming several roles at once without even realizing it: storyteller, detective, reporter, historian, teacher, maybe even rebel. Tell them that and they may feel empowered. They may see that with a mix like that at work inside them, it is hard to imagine *not* writing something intriguing. The difference between non-exciting nonfiction and exciting nonfiction is a well-equipped writer.

### Note:

The ideas and tips in this book can be applied to most types of nonfiction writing: reports and factual essays, personal essays, journalism, autobiography, even love letters—though today, perhaps, we should say "love text messages." In the name of simplicity, I have used the word *piece* for any type of writing unless I needed to specify.

Name _____   Date _____

# Pick a Topic

**Goal: Choose a writing topic that excites you.**

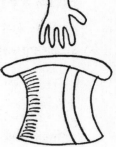

Good writing can make almost any topic interesting. (Yes, even shoelaces.) But at the same time, a good topic can inspire more interesting writing. If you have passion for your topic, you have a better chance of showing passion in what you write about it.

However, don't immediately rule out a topic that doesn't excite you. First, look into that topic a bit more. You may find that you like it more than you realized. Also, don't rule out a topic you know little about—whether or not you think that topic excites you. Challenging yourself to write on an unfamiliar topic is a great way to learn about it—and you might discover a new passion in the process.

**Directions:** Complete the following lists of possible writing subjects. Refer back to these answers any time you are stuck trying to decide on a topic to write about.

| Excites Me/Know a Lot About | |
|---|---|
| 1. | 3. |
| 2. | 4. |
| **Excites Me/Don't Know a Lot About** | |
| 1. | 3. |
| 2. | 4. |
| **Doesn't Excite Me/Know a Lot About** | |
| 1. | 3. |
| 2. | 4. |
| **Doesn't Excite Me/Don't Know a Lot About** | |
| 1. | 3. |
| 2. | 4. |

**Quick Tip**

Something that you find exciting enough to write about can't possibly be exciting to everyone. Your job as a writer is to show why *you* feel it is exciting. Some readers may still not agree, but at least they will learn a different perspective.

Name _____    Date _____

# Find Your Angle

*Goal: Figure out how to write about your topic in a way that readers probably haven't seen before.*

If you choose to write on a topic that's been done many times before, find a new angle on it. For example, the topic "people getting cell phones" may be too common to engage readers. Instead, you could write about people who gave up their land lines (home phones) and now use only cell phones. That is more specific and much fresher.

Or, take Benjamin Franklin. Everyone has heard about his kite-flying electricity experiment, but how many know that as a boy he wrote and published a poem about the real-life pirate Blackbeard? Telling a less familiar story about a familiar person is usually a great angle.

## Part A

*Directions:* For each topic given, choose a more specific angle. If you're stuck, read a little about the topic to see if that triggers any ideas.

| Topics | Possible Angles |
|---|---|
| pelicans | *Do pelicans pose a danger to airplanes?* |
| sidewalks | |
| babysitters | |
| Halloween | |
| cruise ships | |
| Helen Keller | |
| basketball | |
| Japan | |
| medicine | |
| jungles | |
| jungle gyms | |
| the radio | |

**Name** _____ **Date** _____

## Part B

***Directions:*** Now write four broad topics of your own and two more specific angles for each.

| Your Topics | Possible Angles |
|---|---|
|  | 1. <br><br> 2. |
|  | 1. <br><br> 2. |
|  | 1. <br><br> 2. |
|  | 1. <br><br> 2. |

When you need to write about a topic that seems dried up and dull, jot down as many questions about the topic as you can. You may hit upon a great angle to write about. For example, every day you use a spoon, but how often do you wonder where and how spoons are made? Or consider rodeos. Do they take place only in fair weather or sometimes also in rain or snow? (A "snowdeo"?)

Name _____     Date _____

## Write What They Don't Know

*Goal: Try another method of finding your angle.*

Perhaps you've heard the saying "Write what you know." This is another way of saying that when you're passionate about your topic, that passion will show in your writing. This idea was covered in Pick a Topic (page 7).

However, you probably have not heard the saying "Write what they don't know." This is another way of saying "Give your readers something new because their curiosity will keep them reading." Yet another way of saying this is "Find your angle," which you may have covered in the previous exercise.

**Directions:** Read two articles on different topics from a newspaper or news Web site. After finishing each article, write any unanswered questions you have about each topic.

| Questions After Article 1 (_____) |
| Title |
|---|
| 1. |
| 2. |
| 3. |
| 4. |
| 5. |

| Questions After Article 2 (_____) |
| Title |
|---|
| 1. |
| 2. |
| 3. |
| 4. |
| 5. |

Could any of your questions become the angle for a piece of writing of your own?

You should not *always* "write what you know." Part of the fun in writing nonfiction is learning from your research. It is a joy to make little discoveries, and you will get more joy as you pass them on to your readers.

*Quick Nonfiction Writing Activities That Really Work!* © 2009 by Marc Tyler Nobleman, Scholastic Teaching Resources

**Name** _____ **Date** _____

# Begin Your Research Rampage

*Goal: Train yourself to hunt for facts in multiple ways.*

Even the simplest things have a story behind them—from magic markers to monkey bars. Researching means finding out as much as you can about your topic—and that means looking in as many places as possible. It's detective work! Maybe you'll even uncover a fact that no one else has.

***Directions:*** Two topics are given. For each, write three ways you can research it. (Example: For magic markers, you can read an encyclopedia article, check a Web site about how the magic markers are made, and call a magic marker company to interview an employee.) Then, write two topics of your own and do the same.

| Topic 1: Animated Movies | Your Topic 1: _____ |
|---|---|
| 1. | 1. |
| 2. | 2. |
| 3. | 3. |
| **Topic 2: Snack Food** | **Your Topic 2:** _____ |
| 1. | 1. |
| 2. | 2. |
| 3. | 3. |

A source list (sometimes called a bibliography) is a list of all the books, articles, Web sites, and other places you took facts from for your piece. With some types of nonfiction, such as essays, writers typically include a source list at the end. With others, such as newspaper stories, they don't. Keep track of where you got every single fact you use, even if you won't be including a source list. You never know when someone will ask you where a particular fact came from.

Plenty of books and Web sites offer tips on writing bibliographies.

Name _____ Date _____

# Check Facts Twice

***Goal: Double-check your facts.***

Fact sources are like gloves—not so great if you have only one. Before using any fact from a reliable source in your writing, try to find at least one other reliable source that backs it up. This is because the first source, though reliable, may still be wrong! It will not be possible to back up *every* fact this way, but it is always important to try.

***Directions:*** For each fact given, find two sources that back it up and write them in.

| Fact | Sources |
|------|---------|
| **The capital of Portugal is Lisbon.** | 1.<br>2. |
| **Though some people believe the tomato is a vegetable, it is actually a fruit.** | 1.<br>2. |
| ***The Incredibles* is a 2004 film about Mr. Incredible, Elastigirl, and their super-powered kids.** | 1.<br>2. |
| **The Olympics symbol is five different-colored rings: blue, yellow, black, green, and red.** | 1.<br>2. |
| **As of 2009, the most complete *Tyrannosaurus rex* skeleton ever found is Sue, on exhibit at the Field Museum of Natural History in Chicago.** | 1.<br>2. |

Think of a random fact you know and write it here:

Now find two sources for it ("my mind" doesn't count!):

1.

2.

A "reliable source" means a publication of some kind that you can trust. That includes many books, magazine or newspaper articles, or Web sites run by an authority of some kind (such as an established organization or company, not the kid next door!). For more information about evaluating Web resources, check out this page:http://www.homeworkspot.com/features/evaluating.htm

*Quick Nonfiction Writing Activities That Really Work!* © 2009 by Marc Tyler Nobleman, Scholastic Teaching Resources

# Determine the Point of View

*Goal: Learn the difference between nonfiction with and without a point of view.*

Some types of nonfiction have a point of view (POV) while others don't. This means some pieces contain an opinion while others are neutral—they just tell the facts and let the reader make up his or her mind without influence from the writer.

## Part A

*Directions:* Write whether you think each nonfiction title has a point of view.

| Title | POV or No POV |
|---|---|
| 1. "The Problems With School Cafeteria Food" | |
| 2. "The Invention of the Garage Door Opener" | |
| 3. "Where Bottled Water Comes From" | |
| 4. "Bullies Need Stricter Punishments" | |
| 5. "Why I Now Believe in Ghosts" | |
| 6. "The Story of Pumpkins: From Patch to Pie" | |
| 7. "Should Children Wear Helmets on Swingsets?" | |
| 8. "How Zoos Take Care of Baby Animals" | |

(Answers, page 76)

A piece of nonfiction that tries to change somebody's opinion is called *persuasive*. In a persuasive essay, the writer gives the reasons why he or she has a certain opinion about a topic—and tries to convince readers to share that opinion. Other nonfiction pieces, such as personal essays, may include an opinion but are not necessarily trying to persuade the reader.

## Part B

*Directions:* For each topic given, suggest two possible essay titles—one with a point of view and one without. There are no right or wrong answers. An example has been done for you.

| Topic | With POV | Without POV |
|---|---|---|
| comic books | *"Why Comic Books Aren't Just for Kids"* | *"How Comic Book Writers and Artists Work Together"* |
| rock music | | |
| the Internet | | |
| school buses | | |
| pizza | | |
| parents | | |

# Start Strong: Action, Part I

*Goal: Determine when openings start with action and when they don't.*

Grabbing is not good—with one exception: openings of pieces of writing. You don't have the first page. You don't even have the first paragraph. The first *sentence* of any piece of nonfiction should grab the attention of your readers. (And the rest of the piece must hold their attention, but that's getting ahead of ourselves.) We all like to read about people doing something. One effective way to start a piece is with *action*.

***Directions:*** Write "action" for any sentence that starts with action and add in words or phrases that signal the action. Write "no action" for sentences without action.

**Example:** Julia Banes knew no one was home next door.

**Answer:** *No action.* (Julia is thinking, but not doing anything yet.)

**Example:** A bee stung Howard Vargas on the nose on Howard's first day on the job.

**Answer:** *Action.* (An insect is doing the action with *stung*, but it is an action nonetheless.)

| Sentence | Starts With Action or No Action? |
| --- | --- |
| 1. As the tree toppled, everyone on the field scattered. | |
| 2. Boxing champion Travis Laredo looked as though he had walked into a pricker bush. | |
| 3. The town of Cityville was about to start building a new bridge. | |
| 4. Seven years ago, corn farmers Nancy and Joe Keats planted an apple tree. | |
| 5. "My movie starts in ten minutes," director Albert Rondall said. | |
| 6. The baseball Vicki caught on national TV now sat on her desk, coated with dust. | |
| 7. Wet footprints trailed up the stairs. | |
| 8. Sally pushed Steve. | |
| 9. Halfway up Mount McKinley, and halfway through the night, Craig was the only person who couldn't sleep. | |
| 10. The general read names from a list, and the soldier nodded after each one. | |

(Answers, page 76)

**Quick Tip**

If you choose to use action in your first line, don't feel it must be edge-of-your-seat exciting, such as someone making a winning touchdown or parachuting out of an airplane. Even small actions, such as locking a door or winking, can have big effects.

# Start Strong: Action, Part 2

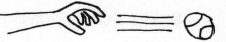

*Goal: Learn the difference between two types of action—active and passive.*

All action is not created equal. The action in some sentences uses the active voice. This means the person or thing in the subject of the sentence is doing something. The action in other sentences uses the passive voice. This means that something is happening to the person or thing in the subject. Whenever possible, use active voice in the first line of a piece.

**Active:** *Sally pushed Steve.* (Sally is the subject, and she's doing something.)

**Passive:** *Steve was pushed by Sally.* (Sally is still pushing, but now Steve's the subject; something is happening to him.)

*Directions:* Determine if the sentences are in active or passive voice. If passive, rewrite them in active voice.

**Example:** The zookeeper was bitten by the peacock.

**Answer:** *Passive.* (Simple rewrite: *The peacock bit the zookeeper.* Rewrite with more flair: *Mistaking the zookeeper's finger for a worm, the peacock chomped on it.*)

| Sentence | Active or Passive? |
|---|---|
| 1. The crowd was asked by police to step back. | |
| 2. The model had her photograph taken while standing under a palm tree. | |
| 3. Bulldozers began to work at 7 a.m., waking up half the neighborhood. | |
| 4. A jaguar whose habitat had been destroyed crept into the village. | |
| 5. In 1803, Meriwether Lewis and William Clark were sent to explore western America by President Thomas Jefferson. | |
| 6. The new variety of squash was taste-tested by food scientists. | |
| 7. Olympic hopeful Shuang Xia practiced four hours a day, seven days a week, for a year. | |
| 8. Sarah Scott's first novel was written while she was in the hospital. | |

(Answers, page 76)

**Quick Tip**

Go with the active voice as much as possible throughout the rest of your nonfiction piece, too. It sounds stronger most anywhere!

# Start Strong: Action, Part 3

***Goal:*** *Turn inactive openings into active ones.*

***Directions:*** Rewrite each sentence so it incorporates an action. You will have to change the wording, which means you may either cut detail or make up more detail, but either way, keep the main idea. Remember, an action is when a person or group *does* something (runs, hides, cooks, cleans, slips, slides, etc.). There is no one correct answer, so get creative! One example is rewritten for you.

| Openings | Rewritten With Action |
|---|---|
| **Books about sharks take up every surface in Barry Jordan's office.** | *Barry Jordan stacks books about sharks on every surface in his office.* |
| **Pirate treasure is supposedly buried somewhere on Buckman's Beach.** | |
| **The wolf howls from across the prairie were a bit frightening.** | |
| **Flowers chosen by the mayor himself lined the walkway to the town hall.** | |
| **None of Frieda Tufts' beauty pageant awards hangs in her house.** | |
| **School buses are parked in front of the school.** | |
| **Police officer Brett Carmichael knew the quickest route to the crime scene.** | |
| **Because of a city ruling, every house on Ford Street must be the same color.** | |
| **The castle has not been home to a prince or princess for 100 years.** | |

If you're struggling to find a way to open a piece with action, make sure you have people (or animals) in the sentence! No matter how hard you try, you probably won't be able to build action into sentences like "The best-selling ice cream flavor is vanilla" or "The rock was more than 500 years old."

## Start Strong: Mystery

*Goal: Try mystery in opening lines.*

Most readers can't resist a good mystery, so planting one in the first sentence is a surefire hook. Keep in mind, mysteries do not need to involve stormy nights, muddy footprints, or broken locks. Even small, quiet mysteries can draw readers in.

*Directions:* For each topic given, write an opening sentence using mystery. It's okay that you don't know what the rest of the piece is about. It's enough to know the topic and the fact that it is nonfiction. There is no one correct answer, so get creative!

| Example Topics | Opening With a Mystery |
|---|---|
| **a girl who raises money for cancer research by training dogs** | *For a month, Dixie felt sick without expressing anything to her family.* |
| **a library is building a new wing** | *The "true crime" section of the library was removed overnight.* |

### Comments

We wonder what kind of sickness Dixie had and why she didn't talk about it. Also, we don't yet know if Dixie is a person—or a dog!

We may first assume it was stolen, only to learn that the library staff removed the books so construction could begin. Singling out the "true crime" section makes it even more mysterious!

| Topics | Opening With a Mystery |
|---|---|
| **a celebrity visits her small hometown** | |
| **prehistoric humans** | |
| **healthy snacks for the holidays** | |
| **poison ivy** | |
| **the Olympics** | |
| **threats to the habitats of snakes** | |
| **how to create greeting cards on your computer** | |

**Quick Tip**

In some cases, you will "solve" the first-line mystery soon after the first line—maybe even in the second line. In other cases, you will want to maintain the mystery until later in your piece.

## Start Strong: Humor

***Goal: Try humor in opening lines.***

We all like to laugh, so another effective way to grab a reader's attention is with *humor*. Fear not—you don't need to be a stand-up comedian to try it. Your regular old sense of humor will do just fine.

***Directions:*** For each topic given, write an opening sentence using humor of some kind. It's okay that you don't know what the rest of the piece is about. It's enough to know the topic and the fact that it is nonfiction. There is no one correct answer, so get creative!

| Topics | Opening With Humor |
|---|---|
| why kids love ketchup | *Kids often leave barbecues with more ketchup on their shirts than in their bellies.* |
| the history of eyeglasses | *We will never know how many camel accidents in ancient Egypt were caused by riders with blurry vision.* |
| moving to another country | |
| the types of clouds | |
| being an only child | |
| how to avoid bee stings | |
| a day in the life of a lifeguard | |
| cleaning up city parks | |
| why kids aren't allowed to vote | |
| how grape jelly is made | |
| camping out in winter | |
| how modern farms use computers | |

**Quick Tip**

While humor can be a strong way to start a piece, it is obviously not appropriate in some cases. If the rest of your piece will not use humor—for example, if you're writing about a tragedy—avoid humor in the opening line as well.

*Quick Nonfiction Writing Activities That Really Work!* © 2009 by Marc Tyler Nobleman, Scholastic Teaching Resources

# Start Strong: Personality

**Goal: Try putting a little personality in opening lines.**

If readers can tell from the first line that a character is happy, mad, sad, nervous, devious, or is feeling some other way, they will be more interested to know what happens to that character. They will want to know why he is feeling that way and whether his feelings will change.

Keep in mind that not every detail relates to character. The fact that a person likes the color green or lives on a dead-end street does not reveal something distinct about him or her. Those details describe lots of people. Try to use details that show how a character behaves or thinks.

*Directions:* Rewrite each opening line so some part of the personality of the person mentioned comes through more vividly. One example is rewritten for you.

| Openings | Rewritten With Personality |
|---|---|
| **William Singleton is in charge of the classic toys exhibit at the Children's Museum.** | *William Singleton took a break from organizing a major classic toys exhibit at the Children's Museum to personally repair a broken jack-in-the-box.* |
| **Until last year, Jennifer Kahala was the personal assistant to tennis star Matt Indeck.** | |
| **The principal of Trenton High School has two high school–age children of his own.** | |
| **Barney Cranston worked in an airport his whole life.** | |
| **The day she moved to Kansas City, Amelia had a pounding headache.** | |
| **Police officer Maggie Nathan is used to wearing her uniform on hot days.** | |
| **While in high school, Hannah Humphry did not know she would become a doctor.** | |

**Quick Tip**

Show personality through what a person says or does, not simply by describing her with an adjective or two.

# Start Strong: All for One (Review)

***Goal: Find the strong starters within opening lines.***

**Directions:** Circle any strong starters in each opening line and write which kind they are—action, mystery, humor, or personality. A line may have more than one kind of strong starter.

| Opening Line | Type of Strong Starter(s)? (action, mystery, humor, personality) |
|---|---|
| 1. When soldier Raoul Tayenga came home, his town threw a parade in his honor—but he forgot which street it was on. | |
| 2. Award-winning journalist Terry Todd spent many years chasing hot stories and one long month being chased. | |
| 3. In 1957, Russia launched a spacecraft whose only passenger was named Laika . . . and was not a human being. | |
| 4. At the base of the volcano, Dr. Charles Bidden heard a rumble and smiled. | |
| 5. The fourth graders wondered less about how much money their bake sale raised and more about the oddly crunchy stuff in Brian Weber's brownies. | |
| 6. When Emily learned she was allergic to peanuts, her mom threw out half the pantry. | |
| 7. John Mullen meant to begin grading his students' history tests on Friday, but didn't get to it until Sunday evening. | |
| 8. At a meeting, Rachel accidentally mispronounced the name of another company. | |

(Answers, page 77)

Keep opening lines as short as possible. The longer the line, the more likely a reader will lose interest even before the period!

*Quick Nonfiction Writing Activities That Really Work!* © 2009 by Marc Tyler Nobleman, Scholastic Teaching Resources

## Start Strong: One for All (Review)

*Goal: Write openings for the same topic in each of four styles.*

**Directions:** For each topic, write four nonfiction strong starters, one in each of these styles: action, mystery, humor, and personality. Some lines may end up involving more than one style, which is more than fine.

| | Topic 1: Amusement Parks |
|---|---|
| **action** | |
| **mystery** | |
| **humor** | |
| **personality** | |
| | Topic 2: Report Cards |
| **action** | |
| **mystery** | |
| **humor** | |
| **personality** | |
| | Topic 3: Trash Collectors |
| **action** | |
| **mystery** | |
| **humor** | |
| **personality** | |

**Quick Tip**

Check the first lines of some of your favorite books. Do they use one or more of the four styles you just used?

# Start Strong: Narrative, Part I

*Goal: Identify narrative in opening lines.*

Regardless of whether you use action, mystery, humor, personality, or some combination of them, you are very often starting your nonfiction with a *narrative*. That means you're starting to tell a short story about a person related to your topic. Nonfiction, like fiction, is about storytelling. Using narrative humanizes your topic, or makes it easier for readers to relate to.

For example, let's say your writing topic is the biggest spring blizzard ever in your state. That is an event, not a person, and we tend to relate better to other people than to weather! Therefore, rather than start with the size of the snowflakes or some other detail about an inanimate object, you might start with a story about someone who had already put his winter coat in storage and had to shovel his driveway wearing three sweaters.

## Part A

*Directions:* Choose one issue each of any two magazines such as *Time*, *National Geographic*, or *Sports Illustrated*, or these magazines' kids' editions. On the lines below, rewrite the first lines of the first five articles, then checkmark each one that begins with a narrative.

Once you've chosen, see how many of your picks involve a narrative—a story about a person or about people.

## Articles from _____ Magazine

| Topic of Article | First Line | Narrative? |
|---|---|---|
|  | 1. |  |
|  | 2. |  |
|  | 3. |  |
|  | 4. |  |
|  | 5. |  |

 *Quick Nonfiction Writing Activities That Really Work!* © 2009 by Marc Tyler Nobleman, Scholastic Teaching Resources

Name _____ Date _____

## Articles from _____ Magazine

| Topic of Article | First Line | Narrative? |
|---|---|---|
|  | 1. |  |
|  | 2. |  |
|  | 3. |  |
|  | 4. |  |
|  | 5. |  |

Are you surprised that the writer of any of these articles was able to start with a narrative? (In other words, did you think there were some topics that could not be introduced by a narrative?)

## Part B

Now choose one of the magazines. Go through the rest of it. Count first the total number of stories, then the number of stories that begin with a narrative.

**A.** Number of stories total _____

**B.** Number of stories beginning with narrative _____

**C.** Divide the number in B by the number in A to get the percent of stories beginning with narrative in the magazine. _____%

It is not necessarily enough to start with a narrative. Some narratives are dull! It is usually effective to start with a narrative that involves one of the suggestions already covered: action, mystery, humor, or personality.

# Start Strong: Narrative, Part 2

**Goal:** *Select the stronger opening from a choice of two.*

**Directions:** In each example, two possible openings to the same nonfiction piece are given. Circle the one you think draws the reader in with more originality. List the reasons you chose this one. Though there are no right or wrong answers, you may find that one seems to hook you more convincingly.

| Topic | Opening 1 | Opening 2 |
|---|---|---|
| auditioning for a Broadway show | *Hoping to land a role in a new musical, Roger Thorn got in a line that snaked down the street.* | *Hoping to land a role in a new musical, Roger Thorn woke at 3 a.m. so he could be first in line.* |
| **Reason(s) for Your Choice** | | |
| | | |

| Topic | Opening 1 | Opening 2 |
|---|---|---|
| action figures | *The first action figures were made of wood and had little detail.* | *The first action figure Margaret got was made of wood and was handed down from her brother.* |
| **Reason(s) for Your Choice** | | |
| | | |

| Topic | Opening 1 | Opening 2 |
|---|---|---|
| nature photography | *Growing up, Petra couldn't sleep without a nightlight, and as an adult she does most of her job by moonlight.* | *Some nature photographers specialize in night photography, where they must be comfortable working with little or no light.* |
| **Reason(s) for Your Choice** | | |
| | | |

| Topic | Opening 1 | Opening 2 |
|---|---|---|
| the design of the American flag | *Historian Bob Jackson said the American flag has had several designs over the last 250 years.* | *When Jerry Norton found an American flag with only 40 stars in his attic, he assumed it was a fake.* |
| **Reason(s) for Your Choice** | | |
| | | |

Name _____    Date _____

# Start Strong: Narrative, Part 3

*Goal: Try narrative in opening lines.*

**Directions:** Write two openings for each of the three topics given. Use narrative in one but not both. Ask a classmate (or, even better, a friend who is unfamiliar with this exercise) to pick the opening from each pair that grabs his or her attention more.

| Topic 1: People With Blonde Hair | |
|---|---|
| Opening 1 | |
| Opening 2 | |
| **Topic 2: Laptop Computers** | |
| Opening 1 | |
| Opening 2 | |
| **Topic 3: Watermelons** | |
| Opening 1 | |
| Opening 2 | |

Now that you've tried writing one narrative opening for each of these topics, try writing a different narrative opening for one of the same topics.

| Topic From Above _____ | |
|---|---|
| Alternative Narrative Opening | |

If your classmate liked the narrative openings better, you've got a great tool to use in your next nonfiction writing piece!

Name _____ Date _____

# Include Memorable Details

**Goal: Learn the difference between a detail and a memorable detail.**

Using detail (whether related to action, mystery, humor, or personality) in a first line is smart. Using *memorable* detail in a first line is smarter. To make a first line memorable, the detail should feel new to readers. (Actually, this goes for *any* line in any piece!)

For example, say you are writing about a person who is running for U.S. president. Smartly, you use action, but not so smartly, you use an action we've all seen before:

> *While running for president, Gwen Lynnwood kissed a lot of babies.*

Yawn. The action of kissing babies is indeed a detail, but presidential candidates kiss babies all the time, so it's not a memorable detail. How about this?

> *While running for president, Gwen Lynnwood shook a baby's hand.*

This contains action, possibly humor, and a bit of mystery—readers will be eager to find out why she did something as unusual as shake a baby's hand.

**Directions:** Rewrite each opening line to make it more memorable. You can either change a detail or add a new one. (In this exercise, the detail you add does not need to be factual. However, in your own nonfiction, *every* detail must be true!)

| Opening Line | Rewritten More Memorably |
|---|---|
| **More than 50 percent of high school students don't get enough sleep.** | |
| **Steel mills used to be the only kind of business in Hinksville.** | |
| **The World Wide Web contains millions of pages of content.** | |
| **In the 1700s, European sailors often did not eat enough vegetables at sea.** | |
| **Giraffes live in Africa.** | |

Don't feel pressured to find an interesting detail and build a nonfiction piece around it. Instead, choose a topic that interests you, then look for a little-known or otherwise curious detail about that subject that you could use to start your piece.

# Entice Readers With a Twist

**Goal: Learn how to hook readers with your first line by using a twist.**

A twist is when you take a sentence in a different direction than what the reader was expecting. Twists are supremely memorable. Some people think that twists can come only at the end of a story, but they can also work well at the start.

Let's revisit the unremarkable opening line from page 26:

*While running for president, Gwen Lynnwood kissed a lot of babies.*

Wake up! Yes, the line is still dull. The way it was changed in the previous exercise (shaking a baby's hand) involved a kind of twist. Here's another way to twist the line:

*While running for president, Gwen Lynnwood kissed a lot of dolls.*

We have heard of a presidential candidate kissing babies, but not dolls, so this tickles the mind. What dolls? Her own good-luck dolls? Dolls of kids she met on the campaign trail? Any line that generates questions like these is probably a strong one. Here's yet another way to twist it, this time using a play on words:

*While running for president, Gwen Lynnwood missed a lot of babies.*

Readers will take notice when they see *missed* instead of the expected *kissed*. Missed babies how—she didn't see them in the crowd? She had her own babies back home, and she was wishing she could spend more time with them? This detail creates instant curiosity. It motivates you to keep reading. This kind of twist can be tricky to create!

**Directions:** Twist each opening line so it will grab readers better. Then twist again, in a different way!

| Opening Line | Twist It! |
|---|---|
| **A typical light bulb creates more heat than light.** | 1.<br><br>2. |
| **Emoticons are facial expressions created from the letters and symbols on a keyboard.** | 1.<br><br>2. |

| Opening Line | Twist It! |
|---|---|
| Some people try to fall asleep by counting sheep. | 1.<br><br>2. |
| California is three hours behind New York. | 1.<br><br>2. |
| People have been eating some form of pancakes for hundreds of years. | 1.<br><br>2. |
| Wolves rarely attack people. | 1.<br><br>2. |

A twist should not overdo it. For example, say you started an essay about how dolphins and people communicate, with "The dolphin told the marine researcher, 'We're smarter than you humans thought'" and then you revealed that this exchange is only what the researcher inferred—it couldn't be proven. Your readers would be annoyed because this opening is clearly an attempt to lure them in with something astounding that turns out to be fake.

## Get a Late Start (Pick a Just-Right Starting Point)

**Goal:** *Learn to start narrative nonfiction pieces at the latest possible point in the story.*

Raise your hand if you've heard the phrase *in medias res*. If you haven't, what about the expression "get to the good stuff"?

They mean the same thing, essentially. *In medias res* is Latin for "in the middle of things." Narrative nonfiction stories that start *in medias res* start while a significant action is already happening. In other words, they get to the good stuff right away.

Consider the effect of a piece of narrative nonfiction that does not start *in medias res*:

> *On January 20, 1981, Ronald Reagan woke up. He got dressed, had something to eat, and brushed his teeth. All the while, he talked with his wife. A car picked them up and drove them to the U.S. Capitol. At noon, he was inaugurated as the 40th president of the United States.*

All but the last sentence seem unnecessary to the narrative (not to mention blandly written). They slow down the story. Granted, some people may find the morning routine of a man about to be inaugurated as president interesting, but probably more readers would rather get straight to the inauguration. (Unless, of course, something noteworthy happened in the morning or the purpose of the piece is to show how even historic days include mundane moments. But in either case, the writing would still have to be livelier than it is in this example!)

**Directions:** Given the subject, circle the word in each mini-piece that indicates the point you feel would start the narrative with the most excitement. In other words, show how to get to the action as soon as possible. This will probably mean you are eliminating some detail, but only temporarily—the writer can always go back and give it later in the piece.

| Topic | Mini-Piece |
|---|---|
| **1. Davy Crockett's death at the Alamo** | *Davy Crockett was born in 1786. His parents were John and Rebecca. He grew up in Tennessee. He married in 1806 and again in 1816 after his first wife died. After serving as a U.S. congressman and publishing his autobiography, Crockett headed to Texas, which was then part of Mexico. He went to explore and ended up joining Texas's fight for independence. In 1836, fewer than 200 men, including Crockett, battled a Mexican army of more than 1,400 at a building called the Alamo in San Antonio. The small group defended the Alamo for 13 days, but Crockett and most of his comrades were killed.* |

| Topic | Mini-Piece |
|---|---|
| **2. how an ice cream company president learned she was allergic to dairy** | *The Lickety Lick Ice Cream factory on West Evergreen Street is a brick building with a large painted ice cream cone decorating one exterior wall. Smells of chocolate and vanilla waft from it most mornings. Two hundred people work there today, and hundreds more have worked there since it opened 50 years ago. The current owner, Brenda Halverson, loves the ice cream business but doesn't eat ice cream. It's not that she doesn't like it—she's allergic to dairy products. She found this out as a child—during a school field trip to the very factory she runs now.* |
| **3. how owls hunt** | *Some animals are not afraid of the dark. They are awake when you are asleep. They hunt and eat at night. Some birds fall into this category, such as owls. A barn owl is parked in a tree, swiveling its head around farther than a human can. Though it is a moonless night, it spots movement on the grass below. As quiet in flight as it was invisible in the tree, it swoops down and snatches a mouse with its sharp talons. The mouse is only an appetizer. Dinner will probably be a snake.* |
| **4. the first e-mail marriage proposal** | *Electronic mail, or e-mail, is one of the most popular online activities. Today people assume that everyone else has an e-mail address just as sure as they have a phone number. No one knows for certain who the first person to propose marriage by e-mail was, but it may well have been Charles Munson of Georgia. He and his girlfriend, Clarice Barnes, met by e-mail because a friend introduced them that way. That's why Charles thought it would be appropriate to ask Clarice to be his wife via the computer. They assured family and friends that they would have a real, not cyber, wedding ceremony.* |
| **5. building the Panama Canal** | *For centuries, ships had to travel around South America to get from the Atlantic to the Pacific Ocean, or vice versa. It was a long way around and took a long time. People wanted a shortcut. Central America is a narrow piece of land between those two oceans. Panama is a narrow country in Central America. In the 1880s, the French tried to build a canal through Panama, but thousands of workers died in the process. Some caught diseases from mosquitoes. In 1904, America gave it a shot, and 10 years later, the canal opened. This shortcut has had a large, positive effect on international shipping.* |

(Answers, page 77)

It's okay to tell a story out of order. In some cases, you may start *in medias res* and then go back and explain any other key events that led up to the event you started with.

# Hold Back—Avoid Exaggeration!

*Goal: Learn how to hook readers without hammering them.*

You've learned that some opening lines employ more than one strong starter:

*Principal Caroline Mannis was hanging a welcome sign the day before school started when she broke her leg.*

This has action (*hanging* and *broke*). It has mystery (how did she break her leg?). It has personality (it features a principal who hangs the welcome sign herself). Despite how "packed" the line is, it doesn't overwhelm the reader. Compare that to this:

> *When the principal broke her leg, she screamed, then everyone in the room shrieked, causing everything to change forever.*

That feels too intense (all the shouting) and too grand (the claim that this event caused "everything to change forever"), yet also too vague (what is "everything"?). You know strong starts are important, but this comes on *too* strong, which, believe it or not, weakens its effect.

Try to keep your first lines engaging without exaggerating. Include drama but not melodrama (over-the-top drama). Grab the reader—don't knock him or her out!

*Directions:* Rewrite each line so it hooks readers without hammering them. You are allowed—in fact, encouraged—to leave out certain details. Less is more!

| Opening Line With Exaggeration | Opening Line Rewritten |
| --- | --- |
| A delivery truck screeched around a pothole and tipped over, terrifying drivers and hurtling crates of delicate dishware onto the street and sidewalk. | |
| When Jen Tilden heard that the poor, crime-ridden city would be sending a merciless wrecking ball into her apartment building, she figured life would never be the same for everyone she loved. | |
| The students at Rodney High School were devastated when their football team was crushingly defeated the night before a lightning storm caused a fire that burned down the quarterback's house. | |
| A Wilderness Network crew filmed a lion ripping apart a zebra and pulling out its guts, growling with its large, fearsome mouth and gorging with large, sharp teeth. | |

**Quick Tip**

Though you want your first line to capture readers' attention, it is still only one line. Don't try to tell the whole story there!

**Name** _____ **Date** _____

# Make a Great First Impression
# (Opening Sentences Review)

***Goal:*** *Create captivating opening sentences using any of the techniques you've learned so far.*

***Directions:*** Write ten first lines to ten different nonfiction pieces. For this exercise, it doesn't matter that you don't know what the rest of the piece will cover. Try to come up with ten subjects on your own, but if you get stuck, you can use one of the subjects in the box.

| | | | |
|---|---|---|---|
| volcanoes | martial arts | TV commercials | recycling |
| music videos | Spanish language | crossword puzzles | grandparents |
| fruit juice | car airbags | sunscreen | freedom of speech |

| Topic | Captivating Opening Sentence |
|---|---|
| | |
| | |
| | |
| | |
| | |
| | |
| | |
| | |
| | |

Take as much time as you need to get your opening line as effective as you want it to be. Yes, it's only one line, but that doesn't mean it takes only one minute to write!

Name _____     Date _____

# Avoid Opening Pitfalls: Questions

**Goal: Learn why to avoid starting a nonfiction piece with a question.**

They say that there is no such thing as a bad question. Well, there is *one* such thing. . . .

Starting a nonfiction piece with a question is a weak approach. In many cases, a question doesn't tell the reader anything—in fact, it puts the burden on the reader to come up with a reason to keep reading! You don't want to take readers out of your topic—you want to draw them in.

For example, say you're writing an article about the first time the people of a South American village get Internet access, and you start with this:

*Did you know people in some South American villages did not surf the Web until recently?*

This looks like part of a conversation, not part of a nonfiction piece. Whether the reader silently answers "yes" or "no" doesn't matter. A writer can always find a way to convert an opening question into an opening statement—always a more enticing approach:

*In a small South American hut that does not contain a bathroom, a group of villagers gathered around their shiny new computer.*

**Directions:** Change each opening question to an opening statement on the same topic.

| Opening Question | Opening Statement |
|---|---|
| **Did you ever wonder why the winter sun is not as warm as the summer sun?** | |
| **How many people get the chance to see a sunken ship in person?** | |
| **Why would someone raise bats for a living?** | |
| **Could you identify when Kansas became a U.S. state?** | |
| **Have you heard that some types of chocolate are actually good for you?** | |

**Quick Tip**

Look at the first lines of five articles in a city newspaper, in a small, local newspaper, and on a major news Web site. Do any start with a question? If so, does the question capture your attention or does it fall flat?

# Avoid Opening Pitfalls: Clichés, Part 1

*Goal:* **Learn to root out clichés so that the language in your opening line is fresh.**

*He was busy as a bee.*

*Her bark is worse than her bite.*

*You can't judge a book by its cover.*

You also can't start a nonfiction piece with any of these sentences, or at least you shouldn't, because they're all clichés. A cliché is a saying people have repeated so often that it loses its impact.

When you're writing, follow this simple rule: If you've heard a phrase before, keep it out of your writing. That goes for the whole piece, but especially the first line, where one false move can discourage a reader from reading any more!

*Directions:* Read this nonfiction profile. Circle any clichés you catch in it.

---

### A Cut Above

Vince Thomson makes people happy using only scissors. Now 61 years old, he has been the barber in town since he was 20. He estimates he's cut 10,000 heads of hair, and he has put his heart into it every time.

Like father, like son. Vince's shop was his father's shop before his. It has been in the same spot on Main Street since 1939. "I'm a hop, skip, and a jump from anywhere in town. That is probably why I've lasted as long as I have," he says with a chuckle. "Not because I'm good at my job, but because I'm conveniently located."

His father, Leonard, would joke about all the different hairstyles he saw at work. In the 1960s, the tall beehive hairdo was popular with women. His father didn't like the trend. He always said, "What goes up must come down." It was Leonard's lighthearted view of his job that made Vince want to become a barber, too.

"You do see some strange things," he says. One customer came in all bent out of shape. She said she lost a bobby pin in her long, thick hair. Vince searched for ten minutes before he found it. "It was like looking for a needle in a haystack." But it's all in a day's work, as Vince is fond of saying.

Because many customers like to get their haircuts before they go to work, Vince has to get up at the crack of dawn. However, he likes it. "The early bird catches the worm," he says. "On weekdays, I do almost half of my business before 9 a.m."

He knows that all work and no play makes Vince a dull boy, so he does have a hobby: gardening. "Then again, I use scissors with gardening, too," he says, "only they're called hedge clippers."

---

(Answers, page 78)

**Quick Tip:** Be careful not to confuse an ordinary saying with a cliché. Of course, you've heard the phrase "makes people happy" before, but it's not a cliché, at least in part because it's not clever to begin with. It's just a common observation. That's a funny thing about most clichés—the first time they were used, they actually were fresh! They become tired only through constant reuse.

Name _____   Date _____

# Avoid Opening Pitfalls: Clichés, Part 2

*Goal: Learn how to turn a cliché into an original idea.*

Just as you can convert a question to a statement, you can convert a cliché to an original phrase. It is okay to keep the *idea* of a cliché, as long as you convey it in a new way.

For example, the cliché "woke up on the wrong side of the bed" describes a person who is in a bad mood. There are countless other ways to do this without resorting to a cliché (*and* without simply writing that a person is in a bad mood!). Here is one:

*Star pitcher Brad August scowled as he took the field, even though his team was winning.*

**Directions:** Write eight different sentences that suggest the idea of a person who woke up on the wrong side of the bed. There are no right or wrong answers, and ~~the sky's the limit~~. . . . uh, you can go in any direction you want!

| Freshly Written Sentences (No Clichés) |
|---|
| **1.** |
| **2.** |
| **3.** |
| **4.** |
| **5.** |
| **6.** |
| **7.** |
| **8.** |

This is a great nonfiction writing exercise to try anytime, not just when you're going cliché-busting. Try writing any sentence you're unsure about in at least two different ways to see which way seems stronger to you.

## Avoid Opening Pitfalls: Clichés, Part 3

*Goal: Get more practice thinking outside the cliché.*

**Directions:** Rewrite each cliché into a sentence that readers will not have seen before. To do this, you will have to add new details, such as a character and a specific situation. Any time you don't know what a particular cliché means, you may look it up. For example:

**cliché:** *Curiosity killed the cat.*

**meaning:** *A person who is too curious may get into trouble.*

**rewritten freshly:** *Vicki Stones asked the person interviewing her if the company allows employees to write personal e-mails at work.*

| Cliché | Meaning | Rewritten Freshly |
|---|---|---|
| He felt like a fish out of water. | | |
| It's as easy as 1-2-3. | | |
| Don't cry over spilled milk. | | |
| The two teachers were on the same page. | | |
| You can't teach an old dog new tricks. | | |
| She was as busy as a bee. | | |
| Truth is stranger than fiction. | | |

**QUICK TIP**

You may be using a cliché without noticing it. Maybe you don't even know that a certain phrase is a cliché. To root clichés out of any piece of writing, ask someone else to read it and point out any phrases he or she has heard or read before.

# Avoid Opening Pitfalls: Lists

*Goal: Learn to avoid lists in opening lines.*

Reading a shopping list is boring. In the first line of a nonfiction piece, nearly *any* list is boring. For example:

> *The West Carolina Zoo recently opened habitats featuring giant tortoises, vultures, toucans, and mongooses.*

Did you nod off after *vultures* or *toucans*? Or did you make it all the way to *mongooses*?

To fix a list problem, you will probably have to break it into more than one sentence. For the first of those sentences, use whatever part of the list gives you the strongest hook. Here's one possible fix for the above list sentence:

> *On the latest moving-in day at the West Carolina Zoo, the slowest-moving of the new residents was the fastest to get settled. In mere minutes, a trio of giant tortoises made themselves at home in their new environment. However, both the vultures and toucans seemed nervous about their new cages, and instead of exploring their new habitat, the mongooses disappeared into a burrow for an hour.*

**Directions:** Turn each list into more dynamic writing, using only the items on the list. Don't add new items, or else you may find yourself writing the entire piece!

| Opening With List | Opening Without List |
|---|---|
| **Before closing the library, the head librarian must shut down the computer system, lock the back room, and check to make sure no kids are still reading in the stacks.** | |
| **On opening day, fans streamed into the baseball stadium to find more comfortable seats, a bigger scoreboard, a new outfield wall, and other renovations.** | |
| **A Green Beret's military training includes learning how to survive in the wild, escape from an enemy, and speak a foreign language.** | |
| **German artist Fritz Wolfenstein prefers to work with blue, brown, gold, and yellow paints more than other colors.** | |

**Quick Tip**

Another way to avoid a list is to simply cut out some items. For example, say you wrote "The teacher wore a brown jacket, bright green tie, and corduroy pants." Perhaps focus only on the bright green tie, which is the most unusual detail of the clothing described.

# Avoid Opening Pitfalls: Small Talk

***Goal: Learn to avoid opening a nonfiction piece with boring comments.***

We often ask others how they are doing and they often respond with a simple "Good, thanks." Sometimes we make an observation simply to have something to say, even though that observation may be obvious or just plain boring. Examples of that are "Nice day, isn't it?" and "You look tired" or the ever-popular "Is it Friday yet?"

Some people get stuck in this small talk most every day—which is precisely why you should keep it far away from your opening lines. However, you *can* include everyday dialogue or talk about the weather if it's not the only purpose of the sentence. For example:

*"Nice to see you," convict Mitch Goodman said to the man who helped him escape.*

Although this sentence starts with small talk, it adds a very unusual speaker and circumstance—and that makes it interesting. The sentence immediately establishes that we're reading about a criminal on the loose, which is a provocative topic.

***Directions:*** Label the opening lines that are built *solely* on small talk such as everyday dialogue or weather. If you think the line is interesting even with some small talk, give a reason why you like it. (There are no indisputably right or wrong answers.)

| Opening Line | Small Talk or Something More? |
|---|---|
| 1. "So what?" Teresa said. | |
| 2. "Want more coffee?" asked Garrett. | |
| 3. The clouds shifted, allowing the sun a chance to poke through. | |
| 4. "You're looking good," the producer said to his top movie star. | |
| 5. Elias was sweating even before the southern sun rose and began to cook the town. | |
| 6. Reggie asked his teammate Hank if everything was okay. | |
| 7. "Thank you all for coming," the sheriff shouted to the panicked townsfolk. | |
| 8. Sandra Edwin's husband said, "Looks like rain today." | |

(Answers, page 78)

**Quick Tip**

If your piece is *about* weather, you may, of course, begin with weather—but still, try to make it more stimulating than "The air was warm" or "It was raining out."

# Avoid Opening Pitfalls: Everyday Action

***Goal: Learn the difference between engaging and boring action.***

You've already learned that an active opening sentence is stronger than a passive one. You've also learned that the action does not have to be big to capture a reader's attention—but there is a catch to that. Even if your opening sentence is active, it may *still* be dull if it is an *everyday* action with no additional information given. For example:

> *The soldier sipped water from his canteen.*

Though this line has action, it is everyday action with no additional information. Therefore it is more boring than engaging. Now consider this opening line:

> *The soldier took the last sip of water from his canteen.*

This is still an everyday action, but the line is slightly improved because it now has more information—in particular, information that intrigues readers. They will wonder why it is the *last* sip. Now consider this rewrite:

> *The soldier gave his colleague the last sip of water from his canteen.*

This line is even better. It still has the intrigue about the last sip, but now it also has intrigue about why the soldier is giving it away.

Everyday action (such as drinking water) can have a powerful effect, depending on the context—meaning, depending on what else is going on in relation to the simple act.

***Directions:*** Checkmark the opening lines you feel contain everyday action and nothing more. For opening lines that show engaging action, tell why you found them interesting. (There are no indisputably right or wrong answers.)

| Opening Line | Everyday Action or Something More? |
|---|---|
| 1. The man brushed snow off his shoulders. | |
| 2. The man in a short-sleeved shirt brushed snow off his shoulders. | |
| 3. A small crowd applauded the man playing violin on the sidewalk. | |
| 4. The award-winning photographer's son took a photo that landed on the cover of a major magazine. | |
| 5. At the banquet, the visiting prime minister spilled her drink. | |

| Opening Line | Everyday Action or Something More? |
|---|---|
| 6. At the banquet, the visiting prime minister spilled her drink on another leader. | |
| 7. Astronomer Hanson Giles worked late. | |
| 8. While astronomer Giles Hanson worked late, his family stargazed. | |
| 9. Sometimes a white dog with brown spots naps on our front lawn. | |
| 10. When Ricardo entered the voting booth, he forgot for whom he wanted to vote. | |
| 11. She dropped the laptop but caught it before it hit the water. | |
| 12. He dropped the laptop but caught it before it hit the ground. | |
| 13. My family waved to the newspaper delivery boy as the sun set. | |
| 14. My family waved to the mail carrier as the sun set. | |

(Answers, page 79)

## Quick Tip

If your opening contains an unusual element, you may be able to use an everyday action without boring your readers. Consider these examples.

- *My grandma pulled out a trophy she once won for tennis*. (This is everyday action with everyday everything else, so it could use some sprucing up.)

- *My grandma pulled out a trophy she once won for arm wrestling.* (The type of person and the action are still everyday, but that is okay here because arm wrestling is unusual—at least in connection with both grandmas and trophies!)

- *My blind grandma pulled out a trophy she once won for tennis.* (The person and the type of trophy are not unusual, and this is once again an everyday action. However, because the person is blind, all of the other elements of the sentence become more interesting.)

Name _____   Date _____

# Avoid Opening Pitfalls: Word Choice

*Goal: Learn to avoid certain weak phrases at the start of nonfiction pieces.*

This exercise is not about the content of your sentences (what they are about) but rather the words you use to build your sentences. You do want your nonfiction pieces to start with great content, but also great language.

These phrases bring no zing to your first sentence:

| Phrases to Avoid | Reason |
|---|---|
| **Once upon a time** | This is overused. It's okay with fairy tales, but skip it for everything else. |
| **One day/night/morning/afternoon**<br>**It is/was**<br>**There is/was/were** | These phrases are uninteresting and unnecessary. Always find a way to rewrite a sentence that begins with one of these constructions. |

*One day* (or any other time period) is unnecessary because you can usually remove it without losing any meaning or effect. For example:

- *A jaguar whose habitat had been destroyed crept into the village.*

- *At the base of the volcano, Dr. Charles Bidden heard a rumble and smiled.*

- *Elias was sweating even before the southern sun rose and began to cook the town.*

In each case, you *could* insert *One day* before the first word. However, you probably didn't miss that phrase the first time you read each sentence! This shows that the phrase is unnecessary.

These examples show how a sentence is stronger when it does not start with *it* or *there* and a form of the verb *to be*:

| Starting With "It" or "There" | Rewritten Stronger |
|---|---|
| **It is a fast-moving train, as loud as a jet.** | *The train moves so fast it sounds like a jet.* |
| **There were six ducklings on the front porch.** | *Six ducklings were waddling around on the front porch.* |
| **It was a quiet summer's day when Amelia Earhart's plane disappeared over the Pacific Ocean.** | *On a quiet summer's day, Amelia Earhart's plane disappeared over the Pacific Ocean.* |

Name _____    Date _____

**Directions:** Rewrite each sentence to eliminate the *it* or *there* opening construction.

| Starting With "It" or "There" | Rewritten Stronger |
|---|---|
| There are many young people today who get all their news from the Internet. | |
| It was the pirate way to raise a red flag if they planned to kill people aboard another ship. | |
| There were no surprises in the sequel to the best-selling novel *Vampire Dragons*. | |
| It is scary to think how often some people don't wear seatbelts. | |
| There are red foxes living in cities, eating mice, birds, and human trash. | |
| It was time for the submarine crew to return to the surface. | |
| There were masses of people lining up during the Great Depression, all for a bit of soup. | |
| It is a reporter's job to look for good stories and tell them well. | |
| There are certain plants that are poisonous for humans to eat. | |
| It was in 1948 that the State of Israel was established. | |

One final suggestion about what not to start with: a person waking up. We all start our days by getting out of bed, so beginning writers often start their pieces with someone doing the same. However, the familiar can be dull, so don't start your nonfiction story with a person waking up, unless it is a key point.

*Quick Nonfiction Writing Activities That Really Work!* © 2009 by Marc Tyler Nobleman, Scholastic Teaching Resources

# Find Hooks From Real Books

**Goal: Evaluate the first lines of nonfiction children's books.**

Now that you've soaked up all kinds of knowledge about successful first lines, you're ready to see how well the professionals did. Keep in mind that not every writer would agree with every tip in this book. Ultimately, it's up to you to decide what tips make sense to you.

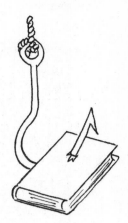

**Directions:** Read the first lines of various nonfiction books and comment on them—what do you like or dislike? If you dislike any, try rewriting them.

| First Line From Nonfiction Book | Your Comment |
|---|---|
| **"You ever hear of the jazz-playin' man, the man with the cats who could swing with his band?"** – *Duke Ellington: The Piano Prince and His Orchestra* by Andrea Davis Pinkney (Hyperion, 1998) | |
| **"The name my parents gave me was Edwin Eugene, but the name my sister gave me was the one that would stay with me all my life."** – *Reaching for the Moon* by Buzz Aldrin (HarperCollins, 2005) | |
| **"Sam Marshall is lying on his belly in the rainforest, his freckled face just inches from a fist-sized hole in the dirt."** – *The Tarantula Scientist* by Sy Montgomery (Houghton Mifflin, 2004) | |
| **"In April 1942, for two days and two nights, a special train, fifty-five cars long, traveled from Florida, the winter home of the circus, to New York."** – *Ballet of the Elephants* by Leda Schubert (Roaring Brook, 2006) | |
| **"U.S. Marines advancing across the Pacific island of Saipan during World War II hacked their way through lush, tangled wilderness and dense sugar-cane plantations."** – *Navajo Code Talkers* by Nathan Aaseng (Walker & Company, 1992) | |
| **"In the days when farmers worked with ox and sled and cut the dark with lantern light, there lived a boy who loved snow more than anything else in the world."** – *Snowflake Bentley* by Jacqueline Briggs Martin (Houghton Mifflin, 1998) | |
| **"Most days, Jerry Siegel slipped into the halls of his high school staring at the floor."** – *Boys of Steel: The Creators of Superman* by Marc Tyler Nobleman (Knopf, 2008) | |

| First Line From Nonfiction Book | Your Comment |
| --- | --- |
| **"Twisters, dust devils, whirlwinds, waterspouts, cyclones—tornadoes go by different names." –** *Tornadoes* by Seymour Simon (HarperCollins, 1999) | |
| **"The cats come from the cracks in the Wall, the dark corners, the openings in the rubble." –** *The Cats in Krasinski Square* by Karen Hesse (Scholastic, 2004) | |
| **"The year was 1763, and in many ways, George Washington of America and King George III of Great Britain were very much alike." –** *George vs. George: The American Revolution as Seen from Both Sides* by Rosalyn Schanzer (National Geographic, 2007) | |
| **"Young Spaniards living in 1492 knew the world was round, but they thought it was much smaller than it really was." –** *We Were There, Too!: Young People in U.S. History* by Phillip Hoose (Dorling Kindersley, 2001) | |
| **"The time is more than a hundred million years ago."** **–** *Raptor: The Life of a Young Deinonychus* by Michel Henry (Abrams, 2007) | |
| **"It began a few years ago with a rock I bought in a small mountain town in Spain." –** *The Story of Salt* by Mark Kurlansky (Putnam, 2006) | |
| **"Pirates are robbers of the high seas." –** *Pirates: Robbers of the High Seas* by Gail Gibbons (Little, Brown, 1999) | |
| **"Long ago, on a farm near the little town of Zezeldorf, Germany, a child and an elephant were born at precisely the same hour as the old church clock struck midnight." –** *The World's Greatest Elephant* by Ralph Helfer (Philomel, 2006) | |

Reading books—and paying attention to how they are written—is always a great use of any writer's time. Good writing will inspire you in unimaginable ways and not-so-good writing will help you figure out what not to do in your own writing.

Name _____ Date _____

# Compare Openings for the Same Topic

*Goal: Compare the first sentences of three books on the same topic.*

## Part A

**Directions:** At the library, find three nonfiction books on the same topic. Write the first sentences of each one below. Comment on their similarities and differences and circle the one you like the best.

**Hint:** Good candidates include famous people, holidays, countries, animals, space, and historical events. Naturally, you will need to choose a topic about which more than one book has been written.

| Source | First Line | Your Comment |
|---|---|---|
| 1. | | |
| 2. | | |
| 3. | | |

## Part B

**Directions:** Look again at the two openings that were not your favorite. Rewrite one of them to make it more engaging.

| First Line (1, 2, or 3?) | Revised First Line |
|---|---|
| | |

Do you find that the more original the book title, the more original the opening line?

Look at two books each on the following subjects: Mexico, mammals, Memorial Day. Do any of them begin with a narrative? A question? Weather?

## Search for the Senses

*Goal: Learn how to incorporate the five senses into your nonfiction writing.*

**Directions:** Both of these short pieces are about the opening of a new town swimming pool. One of the two pieces brings in all five senses. Determine which one and circle every instance. Above each circle, write which sense it is: sight, sound, smell, touch/feel, or taste.

---

### #1

Though the local temperature did not climb above freezing yesterday, the only clothing kids here wanted to wear were bathing suits. They were indoors, of course, celebrating the opening of the town's first Olympic-sized pool, Ruby Pool.

The kids' noses were cold as they walked through the parking lot toward the big poolhouse. Fluffy white towels were stacked ten high along one wall of the locker room. Kids surrounded the pool eager to take a dip. They were given the signal and jumped in all together. The parents stood on the sides and watched.

After frolicking for a while, kids began to slip out of the pool. Most walked across the wet tile floor to pick up a chewy cookie shaped like a pool item. They had a choice of flavors. No one had to tell the kids to wait 30 minutes before going back into the water. They knew that already.

---

### #2

Though the local temperature did not climb above freezing yesterday, the only clothing kids here wanted to wear were bathing suits. They were indoors, of course, celebrating the opening of the town's first Olympic-sized pool, Ruby Pool.

The kids' noses were a shiny red from the cold, but they could still smell the chlorine even before they came inside. Freshly washed white towels, soft as baby bunnies, were stacked along one wall of the locker room. Kids surrounded the pool, eager to hear a bell. When it clanged, they jumped in, creating one large splash and several smaller after-splashes.

After frolicking for a while, kids began to slip out of the pool. Most pattered across the tile floor, now squishy with water, to pick up a chewy cookie. They had a choice of cinnamon diving boards or vanilla life rings. No one had to tell the kids to wait 30 minutes before going back into the water. They knew that already.

---

| Your Choice: #1 or #2? | Why You Liked This One Better |
|---|---|
|  |  |

(Answers, page 79)

**Quick Tip**

Writers sometimes describe a scene using only the sense of sight. In other words, they describe only how the scene looks. Using other senses makes a scene more vibrant and more interesting.

Name _____   Date _____

## Sneak in the Senses

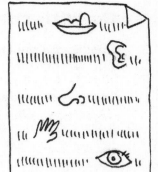

**Goal:** *Practice nonfiction writing with the five senses.*

**Directions:** For each of the first five topics, write a sentence or two that incorporates the senses given. For each of the next two topics, write a sentence or two using any two senses of your choice. Then choose two topics of your own and write a sentence or two for each of them using any two senses. An example is done for you.

| Topic | Senses | Sentence(s) |
|---|---|---|
| **sunburn** | **sight, smell** | *Molly Stitcher couldn't stand the scent of the sunscreen her friend brought to the beach. Now that her skin has turned hot pink like a bubble gum package, she wishes she had used it anyway.* |
| **carnivals** | **sound, smell** | |
| **yogurt** | **sight, taste** | |
| **autumn** | **smell, touch** | |
| **cars** | **sound, touch** | |
| **shoe stores** | **sight, smell** | |
| **bees** | | |
| **bake sales** | | |
| | | |
| | | |

If you wrote every scene using all five senses, it would overwhelm the reader. Mention only two or perhaps three senses in any given scene, unless you feel you can fit in more without overloading on description.

# Go With the Show (Don't Tell!), Part I

**Goal:** *Learn the importance of showing as opposed to telling in nonfiction writing.*

One of the most-repeated pieces of writing advice is "show, don't tell." Though writers often say this about fiction, it is also important with nonfiction.

*Telling* means a writer is spelling out what is happening with a straightforward description. For example:

> *Paleontologist Henry Hanson was hot and afraid.* (This says how Henry feels, both physically—hot—and in his mind—afraid.)

*Showing* means a writer is using action, dialogue, or a character's thoughts to describe what is happening:

> *Sweat glued Dr. Henry Hanson's T-shirt to his body. He tugged the brim of his hat down to cover more of his face. Every time he glanced behind him, he dug a little faster. He didn't want to damage the bone he was unearthing, but he also didn't want to still be in that part of the desert after dark.*

or

> *"It's not supposed to be 90 degrees this time of year," Dr. Mallory Peake said as she and Dr. Henry Hanson worked on their paleontological site.*
>
> *"I can't believe you're thinking about the temperature right now," said Dr. Hanson, wiping his brow with his sand-coated arm. "Those hostile nomads could return at any moment."*
>
> *"They're probably sitting in an air-conditioned tent somewhere," Dr. Peake replied, "like I wish we were doing."*

Each rewrite conveys the same idea that "Henry Hanson was hot and afraid," but does it in a more dynamic way. In the first version, the showing is done with action and thoughts. In the second version, the showing is done largely with dialogue.

When a writer shows instead of tells, the reader must think a little more to figure out what is happening—and that means he or she is more involved in what you have written.

**Directions:** Turn each example of telling into showing. There are countless ways to do this! Adding action, dialogue, and thoughts are just a few.

| Sentence With Telling | Rewritten With Showing |
|---|---|
| **The school was a low building of red brick.** | |
| **Though the computer was new, it made a loud hum.** | |

| Sentence With Telling | Rewritten With Showing |
|---|---|
| Frogs prefer moist environments. | |
| As a kid, Kevin never wanted to try out for the baseball team. | |
| The Space Shuttle launches like a rocket and lands like an airplane. | |
| The one food chef Pierre Lavenne would not serve was French fries. | |
| Many residents of New York City are originally from other countries. | |
| Matt's comic book collection took up too much space in his room, so he sold some of it. | |
| Robots do not always look like human beings. | |
| Studying to become a veterinarian was tougher than Sean imagined. | |
| Joanne Reamer's longtime goal was to invent a more comfortable bicycle seat. | |

You shouldn't *always* show instead of tell. As you probably noticed from rewriting the examples, showing usually uses more words than telling. If you "showed" every scene, it would get long and sometimes tedious—too much beat-by-beat action or dialogue can slow down a piece and turn off a reader.

# Go With the Show (Don't Tell), Part 2

*Goal: Identify examples of "showing" in nonfiction books and rewrite them as "telling."*

**Directions:** In two or more nonfiction books or articles, find examples of showing rather than telling and write them here. Then go backward and convert the showing to telling.

**Hint:** The purpose of this activity is not to teach you how to tell about something—most of us can do that automatically, and much of the time it's better to show instead of tell. Rather, the purpose is to help you further understand the difference between telling and showing. Sometimes going backward for a moment helps you move forward with even greater skill!

| Source | Example of Showing |
|---|---|
| | |
| | **Rewritten as Telling** |
| | |

| Source | Example of Showing |
|---|---|
| | |
| | **Rewritten as Telling** |
| | |

| Source | Example of Showing |
|---|---|
| | |
| | **Rewritten as Telling** |
| | |

| Source | Example of Showing |
|---|---|
| | |
| | **Rewritten as Telling** |
| | |

# Eject Some Adjectives, Part I

**Goal: *Learn how to describe things without relying only on adjectives.***

Adjectives are words that describe nouns. For example:

- the **quick** fox
- the **nasty** storm
- the **energetic** teacher

None of these phrases give the reader anything new or exciting. Adjectives are easy to use, but often they are a sign of telling rather than showing. Here are ways of rewriting the three phrases above with fewer adjectives and more pizzazz:

- the fox that darted out of sight like a snapped elastic band
- the storm that felt like it was taking bites out of our house
- the teacher who always smiled—and occasionally leaped—in class

Always look for ways to eject some adjectives and replace them with a more original description.

**Directions:** Eject the adjectives and rewrite each phrase in a descriptive way readers haven't seen before. Remember, you're losing the adjectives but not the *meaning* of the adjectives!

| With Adjective | Rewritten With Adjective Ejected |
|---|---|
| the <u>sad</u> child | |
| the <u>chilly</u> basement | |
| the <u>playful</u> chimp | |
| the <u>chatty</u> waiter | |
| the <u>old</u> keyboard | |
| the <u>rude</u> waiter | |
| the <u>spine-tingling</u> story | |
| the <u>loud</u> party | |
| the <u>unusual</u> singer | |
| the <u>breathtaking</u> view | |

Think of ways to describe color without simply stating the color, such as "the blue door." For example, "The door was the dark blue of a newborn's eyes." Or you can sometimes find a way to do this without naming a color at all: "The door looked like a rectangular grape juice stain."

# Eject Some Adjectives, Part 2

*Goal: Find simple descriptions in books and rewrite them in a distinct and memorable way.*

Imagine you're trying to turn the adjective-and-noun combination "a sloppy desk" into a more creative expression. Ask yourself questions such as *What makes the desk sloppy?* and *What else looks sloppy?*

The first question calls for specifics—describe just what is piled on the desk to give it a sloppy appearance. For example:

> *Zigzagged stacks of papers rose like mesas from various spots on the professor's desk. Crumpled balls of paper rested between the stacks. A coffee-stained paper cup stood precariously near the edge, with drops of coffee splattered on the surface around it. In the middle of it all sat what looked like several weeks' worth of unopened mail.*

For the second question, you can compare this sloppiness to something else that also looks sloppy. For example:

> *The professor's desk reminded the student of his own hair before combing it in the morning.*

**Directions:** Look through two nonfiction books or articles in search of a noun described by a single adjective, such as *frisky puppies*, the *scratched plate*, or a *long day*. Ditch the adjectives and rewrite each description in a more vivid way.

| Source | Description |
|---|---|
|  |  |
|  | **Description Rewritten** |
|  |  |

| Source | Description |
|---|---|
|  |  |
|  | **Description Rewritten** |
|  |  |

You don't need to eject *all* adjectives in your writing! Keep some and find alternative ways to express others, particularly the most common ones, such as *good*, *bad*, *fast*, or *slow*.

# Eject Some Adjectives, Part 3

*Goal: Use adjectives in fresh ways.*

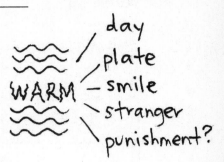

You've been practicing ways to use description without using adjectives. Time to give adjectives their chance!

You have a lot of flexibility with adjectives. Writers love that adjectives can be used in unexpected ways.

For example, we've all heard of a sundae described as "delicious," but rarely the sun described this way:

> *The sun in Mexico looked delicious, like a freshly picked raspberry.*

The sun is something we see and feel, not something we hear, touch, or taste. Yet *delicious* describes a taste. Using adjectives in new ways can mean mixing and matching the five senses. Another example:

*The young computer whiz's leaky shirt kept sticking out from the bottom of his sweater.* Liquids, not shirts, leak, but in this case, the writer is using *leaky* in a fun way to give the reader an image of what the shirt looks like.

## Part A

**Directions:** Below are eight nouns. Choose an adjective that you normally wouldn't use with this noun. Write a sentence with the noun described in this unusual way.

| Noun | Unusual Adjective | Sentence |
|---|---|---|
| rabbit | | |
| belt | | |
| desert | | |
| dessert | | |
| frown | | |
| window | | |
| hair | | |
| secret | | |

**Name** _____   **Date** _____

## Part B

*Directions:* Come up with an unusual noun to go with the adjective given. Then write a sentence with this unique phrase.

| Adjective | Unusual Noun | Sentence |
|---|---|---|
| smart | | |
| broken | | |
| exhausting | | |
| frosty | | |
| thick | | |
| swift | | |
| fancy | | |
| jagged | | |

Think of common phrases that use adjectives in a special way. A "sticky situation" refers to a difficult or awkward event that is not actually sticky, of course—it's just an expression whose meaning we learned from context. Someone once made that up, and then other people liked it and started to use it. Maybe you'll also use an adjective to coin a clever new phrase that catches on!

 *Quick Nonfiction Writing Activities That Really Work!* © 2009 by Marc Tyler Nobleman, Scholastic Teaching Resources

Name _____     Date _____

## Rein In Description

*Goal: Learn how to identify and cut out unneeded description.*

### Part A

*Directions:* Imagine you had to write a one-paragraph summary of Stonehenge and you turned in the one below. Read and evaluate the paragraph.

---

**Big Stones, Big Mystery (original)**

Rising out of the brilliant green southern plain of the United Kingdom is a mysterious prehistoric monument called Stonehenge. The United Kingdom is one of the more than 40 countries of Europe, occupying its own set of islands, some big, some small. Stonehenge is located 8 miles outside the city of Salisbury in the southeast section of the country. Salisbury is also known for its cathedral, completed in the year 1258. Stonehenge consists of large, standing stones arranged in a circle. Some stones also lie on top of other stones, forming what looks like a table. The standing stones are more than 13 feet high. Whoever built Stonehenge had to have a way to move such heavy stones. This was, of course, before the invention of cars or trains, as the first functioning cars were invented in the 1800s and the modern trains were first put to use in the 1800s as well. Historians do not know for sure who built Stonehenge, when Stonehenge was built, or why Stonehenge was built, but they have many guesses. Some feel Stonehenge is a religious site whose original construction may date back to around 3100 B.C.E. Others believe it is a place where ancient people looked at the stars. One idea is that the wizard Merlin moved the stones there by magic. Merlin is a character in the story of King Arthur, and both are most likely fictional. Visitors used to be able to walk up to the stones and touch them, but now the organization that protects the site does not allow visitors to walk near the stones or touch them because that could damage Stonehenge. Instead, visitors must stay behind a rope that rings the monument and look at the monument from there.

---

Okay, we'll stop here. What is wrong with this passage? Perhaps you said it's too long. That's partially correct. It includes too many unnecessary details and repetitive language, which makes it *feel* long. If it contained the same number of sentences but each sentence told a new and interesting fact, and told it in a well-written way, it would *not* be too long!

Let's revisit this piece, revised, on the next page.

## Part B

*Directions:* Here is the piece again, now tightened up. Compare this version with the original and note what was cut or changed.

---

### Big Stones, Big Mystery (revised)

Rising out of the brilliant green plain of the southeastern United Kingdom is a mysterious prehistoric monument called Stonehenge. It consists of stones that are more than 13 feet high and arranged in a circle. Some stones also lie on top of other stones, forming what looks like a table. Historians do not know who built Stonehenge, or when or why they did it, but they have many guesses. Some feel Stonehenge is a religious site whose original construction may date back to around 3100 B.C.E. Others believe it to be a place where ancient people looked at the stars. One idea is that the legendary wizard Merlin moved the stones there by magic. Visitors used to be able to touch the stones, but now the organization that protects the site does not allow that because it could damage Stonehenge. Instead, visitors must look from behind a rope that rings the monument.

---

Certain details were cut from the original paragraph because they are unnecessary. Write three of them here:

| | |
|---|---|
| **1.** | |
| **2.** | |
| **3.** | |

Certain words or phrases were cut because they are repetitive. Write three of them here:

| | |
|---|---|
| **1.** | |
| **2.** | |
| **3.** | |

Be careful not to pad your writing with extra facts. Packing in more facts doesn't automatically make a better piece of nonfiction! Sometimes you may come across a fascinating fact but will have to leave it out because it does not relate closely enough to the main topic.

## Part C

*Directions:* Rewrite this piece, cutting unnecessary detail or repetitive language.

---

### An Unusual Mammal (original)

Some animals live in only one place on Earth, not including zoos. In other words, they are found in only one natural habitat. The platypus is such an animal. This unusual mammal lives along the eastern coast of the country of Australia, which is an island nation whose capital is Canberra. The platypus has not been found living in other areas. Imagine the offspring if a beaver and a duck mated and had a baby that looked like a cross between them both. That is one way to describe the platypus. It has a flat snout that resembles the beak of a duck, though it is a snout, not a beak. Ducks also live in Australia, which is not only a country but one of the seven continents. Also like ducks, platypuses have webbed feet. Unlike ducks, platypuses do not quack. The platypus varies in weight but can grow to weigh slightly more than five pounds. That is not unusual, but two other facts about the platypus are. One, it is the only known mammal that gives birth by laying eggs. The second unusual fact about platypuses that hasn't already been mentioned is that it is venomous. Most other mammals are not. Male platypuses can deliver venom with two small points on its hind legs. The venom can kill small animals but not humans, though it can cause severe pain in humans without killing them.

---

### An Unusual Mammal (revised)

_____

_____

_____

_____

_____

_____

_____

_____

_____

_____

_____

_____

_____

_____

# Choose Details That Make a Difference, Part I

*Goal: Learn how to include description naturally and gradually.*

You've been learning techniques for strengthening your description, such as not relying on adjectives alone. This exercise is also about being more original when writing description, but in more than a single line. Now you will work on writing effective description throughout an entire piece.

## Part A

*Directions:* Imagine you are writing a magazine article about an immigrant arriving in America in the early 1900s and seeing the Statue of Liberty for the first time. Read this version and evaluate the description.

---

### New Arrival (original)

In the Polish village Josef Krasecki had always called home, no structure except the church was more than two stories high. As the crowded ship he rode across the Atlantic chugged into New York Harbor, the 21-year-old craned his neck up at the dark figure silhouetted in front of the morning sun. She stood on a grand pedestal and was taller than anything he had seen. She was cast in copper. She wore a crown with seven spires and a robe. She held a tablet in one hand and a torch in another. She had no expression. She made Josef feel welcome in his new country.

---

Could this description read more effectively? Yes! Now read the revision of "New Arrival" and circle the details that improved the writing.

---

### New Arrival (revised)

In the Polish village Josef Krasecki had always called home, no structure except the church was more than two stories high. As the crowded ship he rode across the Atlantic chugged into New York Harbor, the 21-year-old craned his neck up at the dark figure silhouetted in front of the morning sun. She stood atop a grand pedestal, as tall as six houses from his village if they were piled on top of one another. An arc of seven spires jutted out from her crown, pointing to the heavens. In one hand, she clutched a tablet close to her breast. In the other, she held a glorious torch straight up. Josef imagined it could glow so strong that even his loved ones back home might be able to see it on dark nights. Cast fully in copper and draped in a robe of many folds, the statue wore a mysterious expression—maybe peaceful, maybe protective. Even though she wasn't looking at him, Josef felt that she was welcoming him to this strange, faraway land.

---

The description of the Statue of Liberty in the original is not riveting writing—it's just a list. Description can be deadly dull if told in a straightforward manner. Your prescription when writing description: *Dazzle, don't drone.* Sometimes this requires more words, but in the end, the piece will read better, so it's a fair trade-off! On the next page, you'll tackle the revision of two dry, list-like descriptions.

Name _____  Date _____

## Part B

*Directions:* Rewrite each piece, incorporating the description more naturally.

Lake Mellow has quite a history. People have come here to swim, to fish, to take photographs, or to canoe. Lake Mellow is big. It is half a mile wide and just over a mile long. It is surrounded by trees. Some are fir trees. Some are maple or birch trees. There is a small beach in one section. The beach has a small pier. Sometimes the water looks blue. Sometimes it looks brown.

_____

_____

_____

_____

The tiger isn't the animal nicknamed "king of the beasts"—but it could be. Tigers are big cats and fierce meat-eaters. They prey on animals big and small, including deer, boars, monkeys, fish, and even elephants. The only predator capable of taking down a tiger is a human (with a gun). Tigers commonly have orange and black striped fur. They have long hind legs and large paws. Some live in warm, leafy jungles. Others live in snowy forests. Tigers may be strong, fast, and dangerous, but they generally avoid humans.

_____

_____

_____

_____

_____

When describing something, focus only on the most notable details. You don't have to mention every article of clothing a person is wearing or every feature of a building.

Name _____ Date _____

## Choose Details That Make a Difference, Part 2

*Goal: Rewrite simple descriptions from books in a different way.*

*Directions:* Look through several nonfiction books or articles in search of a description that is more than just an adjective. Rewrite each description in a different way—also using more than adjectives. You may use the same source to select more than one description.

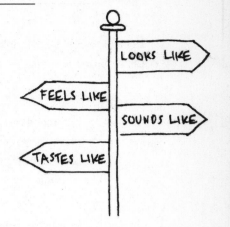

| Source | Description | Description Rewritten |
|---|---|---|
|  |  |  |
|  |  |  |
|  |  |  |
|  |  |  |
|  |  |  |

This activity is not suggesting that the descriptions by these authors need improving. (Sometimes simple is good, and sometimes a little more creativity is called for!) Rather, the purpose of this exercise is to show that a writer can often find multiple ways to describe something.

Name _____    Date _____

# Give Sentences a Fresh Start

***Goal: Learn to vary sentence structure.***

By now you may well be an ace at beginning a nonfiction piece strongly. But what about the rest of the beginnings in your piece—the first word of all the *other* lines?

Don't panic. You don't need to make every single line in a piece as memorable as the first, but you do have to pay attention to how each line starts. To be specific, you want the words that begin each line to vary. If they don't, it will read like this:

> *Neil Armstrong was the first man to walk on the moon. He and two other astronauts flew there in July 1969. He and Buzz Aldrin, one of the other two astronauts, landed the lunar module on the surface as the world watched. He stepped onto the moon and said, "That's one small step for man, one giant leap for mankind." He was soon joined by Aldrin. He and Aldrin collected soil, took photographs, and planted a flag on the surface. He made no other spaceflights after that.*

All but the first sentence begin with *He*. Even though the subject is gripping, the piece starts to read like the sound of water dripping—repetitive and annoying! To fix it, start the lines in different ways as much as possible. For example:

> *Neil Armstrong was the first man to walk on the moon. In July 1969, he and two other astronauts flew there. As the world watched, Armstrong and Buzz Aldrin, one of the other two astronauts, landed the lunar module on the surface. Stepping onto the moon, Armstrong said ,"That's one small step for man, one giant leap for mankind." Aldrin soon joined Armstrong. The two astronauts collected soil, took photographs, and planted a flag on the surface. Armstrong made no other spaceflights after that.*

Notice how the sentences in the revised piece use the following techniques to vary the sentence structure:

- Begin with prepositional phrases, such as *In July 1969* and *As the world watched.*

- Rename a repeated subject: Neil Armstrong is referred to by his full name the first time he is named, but by his last name only or as *he* in the rest of the piece.

- Change the subject: *He was soon joined by Aldrin* can be changed to a stronger, active sentence with Aldrin as the subject: *Aldrin soon joined Armstrong.*

On the next page, it's your turn to tackle repetitive sentences.

This is not to say you can never begin two lines in a piece the same way—that would be next to impossible! However, at the least, try to avoid beginning any two consecutive lines the same way.

**Directions:** Rewrite these passages so that the sentence structure is not repetitive.

In 1950, a comic strip named *Peanuts* debuted. It was created, written, and drawn by cartoonist Charles M. Schulz. It featured a lovable loser named Charlie Brown and his clever dog, Snoopy. It also featured Charlie Brown's good friend Linus, Linus's crabby sister Lucy, and baseball star Peppermint Patty. It became one of the most famous comic strips in history. It inspired animated TV shows, books, toys, songs, greeting cards, balloons in the Macy's Thanksgiving parade, and even a Broadway musical. It ran uninterrupted until 2000.

_____

_____

_____

_____

_____

_____

You don't need to live in fear of lightning because relatively few people a year are struck. You should, however, learn lightning safety. You should go inside a fully enclosed building at the first sign of lightning, even if it is not raining yet. You could also go into a car with all windows closed. You should not consider pavilions or tents safe. You should not go in or near water. You should not be the tallest thing in the area, so if you are in an open field with no shelter nearby, crouch down and duck your head between your knees. You should not lie down. You should not touch metal. If indoors, you should avoid using electrical devices.

_____

_____

_____

_____

_____

_____

# Add Suspense, Part 1

**Goal: *Learn how to create a cliffhanger.***

Some stories (in books, magazines, film, or TV) stop right in the middle of an exciting moment. Then you read or hear "To be continued…" and have to wait a week, a month, or sometimes longer to find out what happens next. In one such chapter of a novel from the 1800s, the exciting moment was a person hanging off the edge of a cliff. This, as you probably just figured out, is where the term *cliffhanger* comes from.

Cliffhangers add a thrill to your nonfiction writing. They entice readers into wanting to read more of your piece. They can be a nerve-wracking moment (like a person hanging off a cliff) or a quiet yet suspenseful moment (like a person opening a letter from a person she hasn't seen in 20 years).

Here are some examples of cliffhangers that could be used to end an entire piece, a chapter, or a section within a chapter:

- *The dam inspectors failed to notice that a crack was forming.* (Readers will want to find out if the dam eventually bursts.)

- *The campers realized the sound outside their tent came from a grizzly bear.* (Readers will want to find out if the bear attacks.)

- *As she was about to announce the winner, someone rushed over and whispered in her ear.* (Readers will want to find out what the person whispered.)

**Directions:** Imagine you're writing a nonfiction book on each of the topics. Write a cliffhanger you could use to end one chapter and entice readers to read the next chapter.

| Topic | Cliffhanger |
|---|---|
| **cowboys** | |
| **gym class** | |
| **computer viruses** | |
| **jellyfish** | |

Like other writing techniques, the cliffhanger loses punch if used too much. Save cliffhangers for when you most need to grab hold of your readers and hurl them into the next part of your piece.

Name _____  Date _____

# Add Suspense, Part 2

*Goal: Study cliffhangers in books.*

**Directions:** Survey the nonfiction books on your bookshelf (or the library's) and look for four cliffhangers that you like. Your best chance of finding cliffhangers might be in history books. Look for cliffhangers at the end of a chapter or a section. Write them here and explain why you like each one.

| Cliffhanger | Why You Like It |
|---|---|
|  |  |
|  |  |
|  |  |
|  |  |

If you can think of any cliffhangers you've read elsewhere, write them here (or describe them, if you don't have access to the particular book).

| Cliffhanger | Source |
|---|---|
|  |  |
|  |  |
|  |  |

When trying to craft your own cliffhangers, referring back to this page may trigger an original idea for your own writing.

Name _____    Date _____

# End Sentences With Impact, Part I

***Goal:*** *Learn how to construct a sentence so the most interesting part comes last.*

Which version of this sentence from a nonfiction piece reads better to you?

- *From the back of the courtroom, a man stood and shouted at the judge.*

- *A man stood and shouted at the judge from the back of the courtroom.*

Either sentence is perfectly fine, but the first sentence is stronger in one sense: It puts the "engine" of the sentence—the part from which it gets its power—at the end. In this case, it is more compelling to know what the man did rather than where he was. When a writer puts the engine last, he's creating a mini-cliffhanger. It keeps the reader moving fast into the next sentence.

> *The medic knew he had to perform surgery in the middle of the battlefield even though the injured soldier said he felt fine.*

Surgery during battle is a more dramatic element than a soldier saying he feels fine. Therefore, that is the idea that works best at the end of the sentence, like this:

> *Even though the injured soldier said he felt fine, the medic knew he had to perform surgery in the middle of the battlefield.*

***Directions:*** Determine which sentences have their most powerful part at the end. Checkmark those sentences. Rewrite the weaker sentences so their engine comes last.

**Hint:** Different people may feel differently about what the engine is. Also, some sentences may have more than one engine! Therefore, there is no single right or wrong answer for each.

| Sentence | Okay or Rewrite? |
|---|---|
| Jesse James, who became notorious for his daring train robberies, was born in Missouri. |  |
| Four crew members were stung by wasps while filming the latest *Oklahoma Smith* adventure movie. |  |
| The investigator peered into the attic expecting to see a valuable, long-lost statue, not just piles of musty clothes. |  |

| Sentence | Okay or Rewrite? |
|---|---|
| An unknown, unarmed man stood alone in front of advancing Chinese tanks while a large crowd watched. | |
| A day before the earthquake rattled the city without warning, the governor and his family happened to leave for vacation. | |
| Two young girls shocked the world by taking photographs of what they claimed were real fairies dancing in the woods. | |
| Leading entomologist Carl Milligan announced his discovery of a new—and blue—species of cricket in a speech at the National Bug Conference. | |
| Even though he was staying alone, the businessman heard someone's cell phone ring as he entered his hotel room. | |
| During gladiator fights in ancient Rome, the crowd helped decide a gladiator's fate by using hand gestures to show if they wanted him to live or die. | |
| Several surfers helped with the rescue effort of a young beached whale before returning to the waves themselves. | |

Not every sentence has an engine. Some sentences are there simply to convey information, and there is no intrigue involved. For example, "The woman walked up and down the aisles while talking on her cell phone." Neither walking up and down aisles nor talking on a cell phone is more intriguing than the other. Either action, however, could be intriguing depending on the context—for example, if we know the woman is an undercover police officer.

Name _____   Date _____

# End Sentences With Impact, Part 2

*Goal:* **Write your own sentences with the engine at the end.**

*Directions:* Choose eight nonfiction topics that interest you and write
a sentence about each in which the engine is at the end. These don't
have to be the opening sentence of a piece. By all means, use reference
material to get your facts straight or even to generate an idea.

| Topic | Sentence Written With Engine at the End |
|---|---|
| **1.** | |
| **2.** | |
| **3.** | |
| **4.** | |
| **5.** | |
| **6.** | |
| **7.** | |
| **8.** | |

You don't need to map out the sentence in your head before you write. Simply
write it as it comes to you, then go back and analyze it once it's on paper. That can
make it easier to figure out what the engine is, if any.

Name _____ Date _____

# Quote Them on That: Interviewing, Part I

***Goal: Learn how to prepare a list of people to interview.***

Name almost any topic and someone will have an opinion about it. Other people's comments remind readers that there is always more than one way to think about a topic.

To demonstrate both points, imagine writing a piece on how a copy machine works. At first, you may be stumped on how to turn it into something more exciting than an owner's manual—first the machine does this, then it does this, and finally it does this. To work in a human angle, simply find a human and ask his or her opinion. One person might say she couldn't do her job without copy machines. Another might say he finds them too wasteful since they use a lot of paper. These comments don't explain how copy machines work, but if they are sprinkled throughout the piece, they will brighten it up overall.

Quotations from other people make nonfiction sparkle—especially original quotations. By using quotations from interviews you conduct yourself, you're giving readers ideas they definitely have not seen anywhere before.

***Directions:*** Name two types of people you could interview if you were writing on each of the topics given. Choose people who would probably have different points of view.

| Topic | Types of People to Interview |
|---|---|
| bald eagles | 1.<br>2. |
| downloading music | 1.<br>2. |
| flu vaccines | 1.<br>2. |
| school uniforms | 1.<br>2. |

Using a quotation to lead a piece you're writing is an example of one of the strong starters: personality. Be sure any quotation you use is worth quoting. "I like copy machines" doesn't say anything, but "I've noticed that people are using the copy machine much less and instead are sending material by e-mail" is a meaty statement that informs the reader.

Name _____    Date _____

# Quote Them on That: Interviewing, Part 2

*Goal: Learn how to write good interview questions.*

Only *some* of the responsibility for getting great answers in interviews lies with the person answering questions. The rest of the responsibility lies with the person asking questions—you!

To improve your chances of getting great answers, ask great questions. This means you need to write at least some in advance of your interview. More questions will probably come to you during the interview, but if not, you'll still have enough to go on. (See the checklist below for some basic questioning tips.)

*Directions:* For each topic given, write five questions you could ask an expert on the subject. Then choose your own topic and write five interview questions for that.

| Topic: Waterskiing |
| --- |
| 1. |
| 2. |
| 3. |
| 4. |
| 5. |

| Topic: Prisons |
| --- |
| 1. |
| 2. |
| 3. |
| 4. |
| 5. |

| Your Topic: _____ |
| --- |
| 1. |
| 2. |
| 3. |
| 4. |
| 5. |

## ⭐ Interview Question Checklist

✔ Keep questions short and clearly stated. ("Can you explain the first step of …?")

✔ Keep questions open-ended. (Instead of "Do you like the new law?" ask "What do you think of the new law?" It forces the interviewee to express his or her opinion more fully.)

✔ Anytime the person you are interviewing does answer simply "yes" or "no," follow up with "Why is that?" or "Could you please explain further?"

✔ Don't be afraid to ask tough questions.

✔ When your topic allows, ask a diverse set of questions.

# Quote Them on That: Interviewing, Part 3

*Goal: Learn how to conduct and follow up on an interview.*

If you've ever asked a question, you can do an interview! Once you have
your interview recorded on a digital recorder or cassette, transcribe it
(play it back and write it down)—yes, this can take awhile. Then you must decide which quotations to
use in your piece. It could be a tough choice—you'll probably have more good ones than will fit.

Here are some useful interview tips:

• Be ready (bring your questions and your recording device—with new batteries).

• Be relaxed (this helps the interviewee feel relaxed, and you'll likely get more information).

• Be quiet (let the interviewee do most of the talking).

• Be curious (thoughtful questions bring out better answers).

• Be thorough (cover every issue on your list, and get the person's contact information when done).

• Be courteous (even if you disagree with the interviewee!).

Remember: You may not be sitting at a computer with your fingers tap-dancing on the keyboard, but
interviewing is still part of the writing process.

*Directions:* Practice interviewing someone about a topic of your choosing. Transcribe the interview,
choose the quotations you would like to use in your piece, and write them below.

| Topic of Article | Favorite Quotations From the Interview |
|---|---|
| | 1. |
| | 2. |
| | 3. |
| | 4. |
| | 5. |
| | 6 |
| | 7 |

**Quick Tip**

Don't be afraid to ask a question that occurs to you in the middle of the interview—
it's as legitimate as any question you have written down!

**Name** _____    **Date** _____

# Finish Strong

**Goal: *Use tips for starting strong to conclude a nonfiction piece.***

You don't slow down as you're nearing the end of a race. Similarly, you don't give up good writing as you're nearing the end of a story or essay. A memorable opening lures people into your piece. A vivid ending helps them remember it. If you were arguing a point, such as why school buses should have seat belts, end by summarizing your opinion and, if relevant, giving your suggestions for improvement. This conclusion is called your *resolution*.

If you were not writing a piece with a point of view, you still owe it to your readers to end with *oomph*. Can you guess four great ways to do that?

Did you say *action, mystery, humor,* or *personality*? That's right—the same four strong starters can also work well at the end.

- Action at the end can leave your readers with the same sense of excitement you wanted them to have throughout the piece.

- Mystery lingers in the brain because people can't help but wonder "why?" If you tease readers with any aspect of your topic that is still a mystery, they may continue to read about it elsewhere.

- People remember what they laugh at, so ending with something funny (as long as it does not contradict the tone of the rest of your piece) will help your readers remember your piece.

- A glimpse of an interesting personality at the end will satisfy readers who like to read about other people—which most readers do. (For proof, consider that one of the most successful magazines ever is called, yes, *People*.)

**Directions:** Look through nonfiction books and articles (print and online) to find an example of each of these four elements in the last line. You may find lines that contain more than one element, and that's okay!

| Source | Element (action, mystery, humor, or personality?) | Strong Ending |
|--------|---------------------------------------------------|---------------|
|        |                                                   |               |
|        |                                                   |               |
|        |                                                   |               |

# Share Your Favorite Beginnings and Endings

*Goal: Size up the kinds of beginnings and endings you like best and figure out why.*

**Directions:** Write four of your favorite opening lines and your favorite last lines from books. Study the lines you chose and see if you notice any patterns.

| Favorite Beginnings | Source |
|---|---|
|  |  |
|  |  |
|  |  |
|  |  |

| Favorite Endings | Source |
|---|---|
|  |  |
|  |  |
|  |  |
|  |  |

Do you notice any similarities among the lines you chose?

Do any of your beginnings and endings come from the same book?

**Quick Tip**

Keep a list of books whose first or last lines you like. Refer back to them periodically to remind yourself what a great effect good writing can have on your own writing.

Name _____     Date _____

# Nonfiction, All Together Now!

**Goal:** *Recap what you've learned about strong nonfiction writing.*

**Directions:** Answer each question according to tips given throughout the book.

| Question | Answer |
|---|---|
| 1. Which of these titles implies the piece has a point of view?<br>a) "How People Deal With Animal Phobias"<br>b) "Meadows Are More Important Than Malls" | |
| 2. Which of these lines features active voice?<br>a) *The Native American healer received a visit in the middle of the night.*<br>b) *The bullfighter threw down his flag for the first time in his career.* | |
| 3. Which of these opening lines contains what would be considered a more memorable detail?<br>a) *The second-busiest holiday of the year for most fireworks companies is New Year's Eve.*<br>b) *For this year's Independence Day, the town hired a new company to handle the fireworks display.* | |
| 4. Which of these opening lines is stronger?<br>a) *Do you think it would kill two birds with one stone to own a garage door opener that is also a portable music player?*<br>b) *The Kiwi portable music player was not designed to open garage doors—but Oliver Jackson found out that it does anyway.* | |
| 5. Which of these lines is showing, not telling?<br>a) *The food critic sampled the tuna special by taking one small bite followed by one large gulp of water.*<br>b) *The food critic could not hide the fact that he disliked the main course at the new restaurant Silver Siren.* | |

| Question | Answer |
|---|---|
| 6. In this sentence, which adjective was ejected in favor of a more descriptive phrase—*wet, shiny,* or *crooked?*  *At a car wash, musician Cadence Jones accidentally left his window open a crack, resulting in a violin that looked as though it had been used to paddle down a river.* | |
| 7. In this sentence from a piece about giant squid, what detail would you save for another sentence?  *In 2006, a scientist from the National Science Museum of Japan took the first known video of a live giant squid, an animal that sperm whales prey on, two years after he took the first known photo of a live giant squid in the water.* | |
| 8. What could be improved about this short passage?  *Roy Risk is Hollywood's top motorcycle stuntman. He has been in the business for twenty years. He has also been in the hospital for twenty months! He loves his job but knows the danger. He doesn't mind it, though. He would rather ride bikes than do anything else in the world.* | |
| 9. Which version of the sentence has its engine at the end?  a) *Magician Harry Houdini dangled upside down from a crane and freed himself from a straightjacket above an enthralled New York City crowd.*  b) *Above an enthralled crowd in New York City, magician Harry Houdini freed himself from a straightjacket while dangling upside down from a crane.* | |
| 10. For a piece on how the circus treats its animal performers, which is a better interview question?  a) *Why do you feel the circus takes good care of its bears and elephants?*  b) *Do you think the circus does not take good care of its bears and elephants?* | |

(Answers, page 80)

As you probably can guess, avoid all the opening pitfalls in your last line, too.

# The Last Words

*Goal: Put it all together in a nonfiction piece!*

**Directions:** Choose a topic and write a one-page nonfiction piece about it. If you have trouble thinking of a topic, go back through other activities you've done to get ideas. Also, here are a few possibilities and some room to brainstorm a few ideas of your own:

- a look at a historical event

    *the first flight across the Atlantic*

    _____

    _____

- a look at a current event

    *this year's race for president (or another political position)*

    _____

    _____

- a profile of a person you find interesting

    *Tim Berners-Lee, creator of the World Wide Web*

    _____

    _____

- a description of a place or thing

    *the covered bridge in America*

    _____

    _____

- an essay where you state a belief and give points to prove it

    *why soda machines should be removed from schools*

    _____

    _____

When you're done, put it aside for a couple of days, then look at it again and revise. When done with that, give it an audience—let your classmates, family, or friends read it. Ask their honest opinion—did your nonfiction come alive?

Nonfiction is fun…writing is fun…so have fun writing nonfiction!

## Answers

**Page 13: Part A**

  1. POV

  2. no POV

  3. no POV

  4. POV

  5. POV

  6. no POV

  7. POV

  8. no POV

**Page 14**

  1. Action. (This actually contains two actions—a tree toppled and people *scattered*.)

  2. No action. (This is an observation about how a person looks, with no action happening.)

  3. No action. (This contains the promise of action, but no immediate action.)

  4. Action. (Even though this action, *planted*, takes place in the past, it is still an action.)

  5. No action. (A person speaking is technically an action, but what he says does not describe a current action.)

  6. No action. (Though this does mention a past action, the scene takes place in the present when no action is happening.)

  7. No action. (This is describing a scene.)

  8. Action. (One character *pushed* another.)

  9. No action. (You could say "couldn't asleep" is an action, but that would be a stretch. Technically, no action is yet happening here.)

  10. Action. (Each person mentioned is doing something: *read, nodded*.)

*Tip:* Remind students that even the sentences that do not begin with an action may grab a reader. Perhaps the writer uses one of the other effective ways to start a piece (see pages 17–19).

**Page 15**

There is no one correct way to rewrite the passive sentences as active. Here is one possibility for each.

  1. Passive. (*Police asked the crowd to step back.*)

  2. Passive. (*A photographer took the model's photograph while she stood under a palm tree.*)

3. Active.

4. Active. (*Don't be fooled by the passive construction "habitat had been destroyed." The central action is the jaguar creeping into the village.*)

5. Passive. (*In 1803, President Thomas Jefferson sent Meriwether Lewis and William Clark to explore western America.*)

6. Passive. (*Food scientists taste-tested the new variety of squash.*)

7. Active.

8. Passive. (*Sarah Scott wrote her first novel while she was in the hospital.*)

**Page 20**

1.
   - threw a parade—action
   - forgot which street—humor, personality

2.
   - chasing hot stories—action
   - one long month being chased—action, mystery

3.
   - launched a spacecraft—action
   - was not a human being—mystery

4.
   - heard a rumble—mystery
   - smiled—personality

5.
   - the oddly crunchy stuff—mystery, humor

6.
   - threw out half the pantry—action, personality

7.
   - meant to . . . but didn't get to—personality, humor

   - accidentally mispronounced the name of another company—humor, mystery

**Pages 29–30**

This exercise involves personal opinion. Therefore, student answers may differ than these. If so, have them explain why.

1. "In 1836, fewer than 200 men, including Crockett, battled a Mexican army of more than 1,400 at a building called the Alamo in San Antonio. . . ." (It gives greater urgency to start in the thick of battle than in Crockett's childhood, however interesting that might be.)

2. "The current owner, Brenda Halverson, loves the ice cream business but doesn't eat ice cream. . . ." (The history and description of the factory can be interesting, but not necessary

for the beginning. The humor and quirkiness of the story come from an irony about Brenda, so that is a strong way to start.)

3. "A barn owl is parked in a tree, swiveling its head around farther than a human can...." (Leading with an owl hunt in progress is as compelling as most any chase. General facts about nocturnal animals can come later.)

4. "No one knows for certain who the first person to propose marriage by e-mail was, but it may well have been Charles Munson of Georgia...." (Readers would probably prefer to first learn about the people involved in the story rather than general statements about e-mail.)

5. "In the 1880s, the French tried to build a canal through Panama, but thousands of workers died in the process...." (The first attempt to build a canal through Panama was filled with drama, so that is a promising place to start.)

**Page 34**

## A Cut Above

Vince Thomson makes people happy using only scissors. Now 61 years old, he has been the barber in town since he was 20. He estimates he's cut 10,000 heads of hair, and he has put his heart into it every time.

Like father, like son, Vince's shop was his father's shop before his. It has been in the same spot on Main Street since 1939. "I'm a hop, skip, and a jump from anywhere in town. That is probably why I've lasted as long as I have," he says with a chuckle. "Not because I'm good at my job, but because I'm conveniently located."

His father, Leonard, would joke about all the different hairstyles he saw at work. In the 1960s, the tall beehive hairdo was popular with women. His father didn't like the trend. He always said, "What goes up must come down." It was Leonard's lighthearted view of his job that made Vince want to become a barber, too.

"You do see some strange things," he says. One customer came in all bent out of shape. She said she lost a bobby pin in her long, thick hair. Vince searched for ten minutes before he found it. "It was like looking for a needle in a haystack." But it's all in a day's work, as Vince is fond of saying.

Because many customers like to get their haircuts before they go to work, Vince has to get up at the crack of dawn. However, he likes it. "The early bird catches the worm," he says. "On weekdays, I do almost half of my business before 9 a.m."

He knows that all work and no play makes Vince a dull boy, so he does have a hobby: gardening. "Then again, I use scissors with gardening, too," he says, "only they're called hedge clippers."

**Page 38**

1. small talk—everyday dialogue

2. small talk—everyday dialogue

3. small talk—weather

4. small talk—everyday dialogue

5. Though this involves weather, it also involves a mystery—why was Elias sweating before sunrise?

6. small talk—everyday dialogue

7. The dialogue is everyday, but the fact that the people are panicked is a key piece of extra information.

8. small talk—weather

## Pages 39–40

1. everyday action

2. This is everyday action with a detail that gives it something more—it is unusual that someone would be brushing snow off while wearing a short-sleeved shirt.

3. everyday action

4. It is not a photo by the award-winning photographer, but rather by his son, that appears on a magazine cover. That is an unusual detail.

5. everyday action (we all spill drinks)

6. This adds another level—perhaps humor.

7. everyday action

8. The intriguing detail is that the astronomer's family looks at the stars even when he is not there.

9. everyday action (though a reader will probably wonder why someone else's dog is sleeping on the writer's lawn)

10. everyday action (we all forget at times)

11. Dropping a laptop is, unfortunately, a fairly common incident—but dropping one over water is not.

12. everyday action

13. It is unusual that a newspaper delivery boy would be around at sunset. Papers are typically delivered in the early morning.

14. everyday action (a mail carrier could still be on his rounds as it gets dark, particularly in winter)

## Page 46

#2

Though the local temperature did not climb above freezing [touch/feel] yesterday, the only clothing kids here wanted to wear were bathing suits. They were indoors, of course, celebrating the opening of the town's first Olympic-sized pool, Ruby Pool.

The kids' noses were a shiny red [sight] from the cold, but they could still smell the chlorine [smell] even before they came inside. Freshly washed white towels, soft as baby bunnies [touch/feel], were stacked along one wall of the locker room [sight]. Kids surrounded the pool, eager to hear a bell. When it clanged [sound], they jumped in, creating one large splash and several smaller after-splashes [sight, sound].

After frolicking for a while, kids began to slip out of the pool. Most pattered across the tile floor, now squishy with water [sound], to pick up a chewy cookie. They had a choice of cinnamon diving boards or vanilla life rings [taste, sight]. No one had to tell the kids to wait 30 minutes before going back into the water. They knew that already.

## Pages 73–74

1. b) "Meadows Are More Important Than Malls"

2. b) *The bullfighter threw down his flag for the first time in his career.*

3. a) *The second-busiest holiday of the year for most fireworks companies is New Year's Eve.* (It states a fact that may surprise some readers, whereas the other line probably doesn't. Also, it has a pinch of mystery since it doesn't yet say what the busiest holiday of the year is, though readers can guess it fairly easily.)

4. b) *The Kiwi portable music player was not designed to open garage doors—but Oliver Jackson found out that it does anyway.* (The other line contains both a question and a cliché. This line contains a hint of both mystery and humor. The mystery: Was it accidental that the device opened the garage door? The humor: A music player opened a garage door!)

5. a) *The food critic sampled the tuna special by taking one small bite followed by one large gulp of water.* (This suggests he did not like the food, but lets the reader figure it out. The other line comes right out and says he did not like the food.)

6. *Wet;* describing something as looking like it'd been used to paddle down a river means it is soaked.

7. *an animal that sperm whales prey on;* it interrupts the train of thought about capturing the elusive beast on film.

8. It needs some fresh starts. All sentences after the first begin with *he.*

9. b) *Above an enthralled crowd in New York City, magician Harry Houdini freed himself from a straightjacket while dangling upside down from a crane.*

10. a) *Why do you feel the circus takes good care of its bears and elephants?* This question is open-ended. It asks "why," which requires a person to give an explanation. The other is a yes-or-no question, and one-word answers aren't interesting. Also, it puts an idea into the head of the interviewee (that the circus does not take care of its animals). A question that does not "take sides" will lead to a richer answer.